ALL BOYS AREN'T BLUE

ALL BOYS AREN'T BLUE

A MEMOIR-MANIFESTO
GEORGE M. JOHNSON

FARRAR STRAUS GIROUX
New York

Farrar Straus Giroux Books for Young Readers
An imprint of Macmillan Publishing Group, LLC
120 Broadway, New York, NY 10271
Copyright © 2020 by George M. Johnson
All rights reserved
Printed in the United States of America
Designed by Cassie Gonzales
First edition, 2020
10 9 8
fiercereads.com

Library of Congress Cataloging-in-Publication Data

Names: Johnson, George M. (George Matthew), 1985-
Title: All boys aren't blue : a memoir-manifesto / George M. Johnson.
Description: First edition. | New York : Farrar Straus Giroux, 2020.
Identifiers: LCCN 2019018174 | ISBN 9780374312718 (hardcover : alk.
paper)
Subjects: LCSH: Johnson, George M. (George Matthew), 1985- | African
American gay men—Biography. | Gays—Identity.
Classification: LCC HQ76.27.A37 J644 2020 | DDC 306.76/6208996073—
dc23
LC record available at https://lccn.loc.gov/2019018174

Our books may be purchased for promotional, educational, or business use.
Please contact your local bookseller or the Macmillan Corporate and
Premium Sales Department at (800) 221-7945 ext. 5442 or by email at
MacmillanSpecialMarkets@macmillan.com.

CONTENTS

AUTHOR'S NOTE

In writing this book, I wanted to be as authentic and truthful about my experience as possible. I wanted my story to be told in totality: the good, the bad, and the things I was always too afraid to talk about publicly. This meant going to places and discussing some subjects that are often kept away from teens for fear of them being "too heavy."

But the truth of the matter is, these things happened to me when I was a child, teenager, and young adult. So as heavy as these subjects may be, it is necessary that they are not only told, but also read by teens who may have to navigate many of these same experiences in their own lives.

This book will touch on sexual assault (including molestation), loss of virginity, homophobia, racism, and anti-Blackness. These discussions at times may be a bit graphic, but nonetheless they are experiences that many reading this book will encounter or have already encountered. And I want those readers to be seen and heard in these pages.

Within these pages, the word *nigger* or *nigga* appears, sometimes in full and sometimes abbreviated as n****. The same is true for *fag* and *faggot*, and their abbreviations. I included these slurs in the text in specific ways for specific emotional and intellectual effect. Please use the same thoughtfulness when talking about this book. If you don't identify as Black, African American, or queer, don't use these slurs in full, which can be harmful to others. You can use common abbreviations, like *n-word* or *f-word* instead.

Please know that this book was crafted with care and love, but most importantly to give a voice to so many from marginalized communities whose experiences have not yet been captured between the pages of a book.

I hope this book will make you laugh at moments. I hope this book will make you cry at moments. I hope this book will open you up to understanding the people you may have never spoken to because of their differences from you. We are not as different as you think, and all our stories matter and deserve to be celebrated and told.

With love,

George M. Johnson

ALL

BOYS

AREN'T

BLUE

Baby George with Great-Grandmother Lula Mae

BLACK. QUEER. HERE.

The story of how I entered the world was a foreshadowing.

When my aunt first saw my head full of beautiful, jet-black, curly hair crown from my mother's womb, she ran into the hospital's hallway where my family waited.

"It's a girl! It's a girl!" she yelled, to my grandmother's excitement and to my father's *slight* disappointment. But by the time my aunt got back to the delivery room, and I had been fully born, she realized her quick assumption would soon need correcting.

She ran back out to the family and said, "Uhhh, actually, it's a boy."

The "It's a girl! No, it's a boy!" mix-up is funny on paper, but not quite so hilarious in real life, especially when the star of that story struggles with their identity. Gender is one of the biggest projections placed onto children at birth, despite families having no idea how the baby will truly turn out. In our society, a person's sex is based on their genitalia. That decision is then used to assume a person's gender as boy or girl, rather than a spectrum of identities that the child should be determining for themselves.

Nowadays, we are assigning gender even before birth. We have become socially conditioned to participate in the gendering of children at the earliest possible moment—whenever a sonogram can identify its genitalia. Gender-reveal parties have become a trendy way to celebrate the child's fate, steering them down a life of masculine or feminine ideals before ever meeting them. It's as if the more visible LGBTQIAP+ people become, the harder the heterosexual community attempts to apply new norms. I think the majority fear becoming the minority, and so they will do anything and everything to protect their power.

I often wonder what this world would look like if people were simply told, *You are having a baby with a penis or a vagina or other genitalia. Look up intersex if you're confused about "other."* What if parents were also given instructions to nurture their baby by paying attention to what the child naturally gravitates toward and to simply feed those interests? What if parents let their child explore their own gender instead of pushing them down one of the only two roads society tells us exist?

When our gender is assigned at birth, we are also assigned responsibilities to grow and maneuver through life based on the simple checking off of those boxes. Male. Female. Black. White. Straight. Gay. Kids who don't fit the perfect boxes are often left asking themselves what the truth is:

Am I a girl?

Am I a boy?

Am I both?

Am I neither?

As a child, I struggled mightily with these questions. And that struggle continued to show up in various ways throughout my life. Now, as an adult, I have a much better grasp of sexuality, gender, and the way society pressures us to conform to what has been the norm. I understand how this sense of normality doesn't hold a space for those of us who don't fit the aesthetic of what a boy or girl *should* be, or how a man or woman *should* perform.

Unfortunately, we are still struggling to move the conversation past an assumed identity at birth. And LGBTQIAP+ people are not just fighting for the right to self-identify and be accepted in a society that is predominantly composed of two genders—which would be the bare minimum of acceptance. We are also fighting to survive physical acts of violence. Many of us are not even surviving that. The spectrum of our traumas can be as broad as our identities.

I started writing this book with the intention that every chapter would end with solutions for all the uncomfortable or confusing life circumstances I experienced as a gay Black child in America. I quickly learned this book would be about so much more. About the overlap of my identities and the importance of sharing how those intersections create my privilege and my oppression.

Many of us carry burdens from the traumas of our past, and they manifest in our adulthood. We all go through stages of accepting or struggling with our various identities—gay, straight, or non-identifying. And race and various other factors play a role in how we navigate them. Many of us are always in a state of working through something—always in a state of "becoming" a more aware version of self.

This book is an exploration of two of my identities—Black and queer—and how I became aware of their intersections within myself and in society. How I've learned that neither of those identities can be contained within a simple box, and that I enter the room as both of them despite the spaces and environments I must navigate. In the white community, I am seen as a Black man first—but that doesn't negate the queer identity that will still face discrimination. In the Black community, where I more often find myself, it is not the Black male identity that gets questioned immediately. It is that intersection with queerness that is used to reduce my Blackness and the overall image of Black men.

Because this is a memoir, I'm sharing some of my personal memories with you. These memories are specific to my experience as a kid, teen, and young adult. But they also underline some of the universal experiences of Black and/or queer people. My struggles are that of Black men and queer men and people who exist at the intersection of both identities. That's where the manifesto part comes in. I believe that the dominant society establishes an idea of what "normal" is simply to suppress differences, which means that any of us who fall outside of their "normal" will eventually be oppressed. In each chapter of this book, I'll tell you memories of my experiences growing up and what I think they mean in a larger context of living as a Black queer person.

I grew up hearing the word *nigga*, which was a term of endearment in my home. It's become a term of endearment in many Black families. By the time I was in middle school, I was using the word regularly with friends. It was the thing to do as a thirteen-year-old—that is, to curse and use the *n-word*. We were all doing it. It was how we greeted one another, how we clowned one another. We had different tones and inflections that could tell you the way the word was being used. But never with the "-er" at the end.

We knew saying that word with the hard "-er" meant something different.

By high school, I stopped using it. Surrounded by whiteness, I wasn't going to dare let my classmates get comfortable using that word with or around me. Anytime a white student even tried to utter it, I checked them. White kids love to test Black kids on things like that. Certain Black kids were fighting so hard to fit in, they would let white kids steal that part of our culture just so they could pretend they were accepted in white society.

By college, I was back in a predominantly Black school—back to using the n-word again with my new friends. It was just like middle school, except as an adult I knew I could use it, and no one could say anything to me about it. Truth be told, most professors hated that we used the word. They were of the opinion that the word had too much hatred in it for us to ever be able to take back full ownership, in any variation.

The n-word was the last word heard by many of my ancestors when they were being beaten and shackled—forced into enslavement in a new land. It was the last word heard by my people when they were lynched as a spectacle for white people. "Strange fruit hanging from the poplar trees," as the great Nina Simone would sing. So, for many of my professors who grew up during Jim Crow, experiencing legalized segregation, there was no reason to be proud of that word.

It was during those years in college and right after college that the NAACP and the National Action Network decided that it was time for the Black community to "bury the n-word." There was this belief that if we stopped using it, the word itself would lose its power.

This brought out arguments on both sides, people for and against this action to destroy a word that is so tied to the most painful parts of history in America. I began to shift to the side that thought it was best to bury it. At that time, I was learning how to be "a respectable negro"—with the good grades and a college degree, attempting to fit into white society, wherein I felt I deserved to be treated as an equal. It was important to me that I didn't use that word, because I felt it made us less than.

I felt that our using that word was a bad thing—because white people cringed when we said it. Because certain Black people cringed when we said it. To me, it just didn't make sense to keep using it, especially because it remained controversial. I did what I always did with most things I didn't want to deal with—buried it.

I wasn't just trying to bury the n-word though. In burying the n-word, I was also burying my queerness. If I couldn't see parts of my own Blackness as respectable, there was no way I was ready to see my queerness as respectable either. But now I know that queerness is a part of Blackness, and that there is no Blackness without queer people.

Then, early in 2012, Trayvon Martin was killed by George Zimmerman—and my entire perspective shifted on being a Black person in this society. I saw that the new-age civil rights movement was being led by people who looked like me. People who were fighting for me and other Black children. It was during this time that my unlearning process really began.

My eyes were opened by seeing the shooting of Black people at the hands of police. Seeing the killing of Black children like Tamir Rice at the hands of police. Seeing that it didn't matter whether you were an affluent Black, a poor Black, a child, or an adult. In the eyes of society, I was still a n****. And my love for my Blackness meant that I had every right to fight for my people and every right to take back ownership of that word.

So, I started using the n-word again. I understand now that my Blackness is self-defined and that to use the n-word or not use the n-word is my choice. But it shouldn't be based on the comfort of those who constantly seek to invalidate me. I understand now that there is no such thing as "a respectable negro" in the eyes of society, nor was I ever made to be one.

BLACK.

My second identity—queer—is a journey that I will be on until the day I die, and I honestly believe that. Every day I learn something about myself. I get to sit and look back at all the times my queerness displayed itself, both in ways known to me and unknown to me.

As a child, I always knew I was different. I didn't know what that meant at the time, but I now know it was okay to be that different kid. That being different didn't mean something was wrong with me, but that something was wrong with my cultural environment, which forced me to live my life as something I wasn't. The fact that I couldn't see my full self in Black heroes or the history books was more about the changing of history to spare white guilt than it ever was about me knowing the whole truth.

I learned that kids who saw me as different didn't have an issue until society taught them to see my differences as a threat. Those differences, like being effeminate and sassy, were constantly under attack my entire childhood from kids who didn't even know why I needed to be shamed for those differences. It wasn't them shaming me as much as it was those raising them who taught them to shame others with those qualities. Most kids aren't inherently mean. Their parents, however, can make them mean.

By the time I reached middle school and high school, suppression was my only option. I had become even more of a minority in the population, and I had to deal with the intersection of Blackness and queerness—and the double oppression that generates—for the first time ever. Fighting for Blackness in a white space came naturally to me, though, and I did it every chance I got. Fighting for my queerness, however, never seemed to be a viable or safe option.

I lived in that isolation for all those years in high school. I only saw snippets of queer representation in small television roles. They were rarely played by people who looked like me. But it was never to the extent that I ever gained the confidence to be that person. Thankfully, college opened my eyes to true reflections of myself—in literature, in art, in class beside me—not early on, but right on time. I realized that the things I had always been running from had never left my side. That the things I had been chasing were all just a myth to turn me into something, some*one* I didn't want to be.

In college, I took a risk and did something that was so far away from being queer that it should've put me even deeper in the closet: I joined a fraternity. I was trying to preserve an image of masculinity for myself—something that Black fraternities have run on for years. However, in finding the frat, I found myself. I found brothers with a common experience chasing the same thing. And instead of the universe giving us what *we* thought we wanted, it gave us what we actually needed.

It gave us unconditional love and brotherhood from a shared queer experience. It gave me brothers who could see my humanity outside of my queerness. It gave me the confidence to define my Blackness and my queerness and my manhood and my masculinity, or lack thereof. I got to live in my totality and, for the first time ever, exist as both Black and queer in the same space and be loved for it, not shamed.

QUEER.

I want the words of my life story to be immortalized. I want to immortalize this narrative of joy and pain, this narrative of triumph and tragedy, this narrative of the Black queer experience that has been erased from the history books. An existence that has been here forever.

I've never thought about immortality before. I always assumed that my mortality would be linked to my inability to survive as a Black queer person. I have the deaths of so many people who look like me in mind. From the HIV epidemic, to domestic violence, to suicide, I watch people like me who don't survive the oppression. They become today's news and yesterday's headlines.

I remember being nervous about writing a book like this. I wasn't sure if this was my story to tell. In writing this, though, I realized that I wasn't just telling my story. I was telling the story of millions of queer people who never got a chance to tell theirs. This book became less about having the answers to everything, because I haven't been through everything. It became less about being a guide and more about being the gateway for more people to find their truth and find their power to live in that truth.

I often think about a statement Viola Davis made when she won her first Oscar. Something along the lines of encouraging people to go to the graveyard and dig up all the dead bodies in order to hear and tell the stories of those whose dreams were never realized. Those are the stories she's interested in telling. Although that is valid, I must challenge it. This book is proof positive that you don't need to go to the graveyard to find us.

Many of us are still here. Still living and waiting for our stories to be told—to tell them ourselves. We are the living that have always been here but have been erased. We are the sons and brothers, daughters and sisters, and others that never get a chance to see ourselves nor to raise our voices to ears that need to hear them.

Toni Morrison states in my favorite quote of all time, "If there's a book that you want to read, but it hasn't been written yet, then you must write it."

This is the story of George Matthew Johnson. This is a story for us all.

Left to right: Rall, Garrett, Nanny (center), George, Rasul

ACT I

A DIFFERENT KID

CHAPTER 1

SMILE

I was five years old when my teeth got kicked out. It was my first trauma.

But before I get into that, introductions: My name is Matthew Johnson. Well, realistically, my name is George Matthew Johnson, but at five years old, I didn't know that yet. It all will matter in the end, though.

I'm from a small city located in New Jersey called Plainfield, about thirty miles from the bright lights of Manhattan. You could literally drive from one end of Plainfield to the other in less than ten minutes. It's a compact city with so many interconnected stories. Triumph, tragedy, and trauma all exist within those few square miles. It is a place I once hated but grew to love as my true home. My only home.

My family has been a part of the fabric of this city for more than fifty years. My parents both held down city jobs for nearly three decades and still live there to this day. My brother and I grew up middle class, or at least what Black folk were supposed to think was middle class. With Christmases full of gifts under the tree, my little brother and I never wanted for a thing. We were blessed to have parents who understood what it was like to have the bare minimum, and who ensured that their kids never experienced that same plight. We are a rarity amongst most Black folks, who don't get to have intergenerational wealth like our white neighbors just one block over.

Family came first for us. I grew up with my little brother, Garrett, in the house. Our older brother, Gregory Jr., and sister, Tonya, from my dad's first marriage had moved out by that time. There were also cousins, aunts, and uncles living in Plainfield. Holidays were always a big family affair. For reference, I think the movie *Soul Food* stands as the closest semblance to my upbringing, minus the fighting. Well, maybe a little bit of fighting.

My parents both worked "9–5, 5–9" as we called it. My father was a police officer who worked very long shifts. My mother was the head of the secretaries at the police department and owned a hair salon in town, where she would go in the evenings after her day job.

Some of my cousins used to live in the projects in Jersey City, an environment my mom's mother, Nanny, felt wasn't very conducive to the safe upbringing of small Black boys. Their parents were like oil and water. I can recall one time when their mom and dad visited Nanny's house. Aunt Cynthia and "Uncle" got into an argument over laundry that I learned much later was really over drugs. It then escalated into a full-on fistfight in the upstairs hallway. That would be the last time I saw Aunt Cynthia for years. Nanny knew she didn't want her grandkids growing up in all that. As she put it, "Y'all can run the streets all you want, my grandkids will not." And from that moment, she took them in and put them into school in Plainfield.

Nanny became the caregiver, cook, nurse, and disciplinarian for us all. Nanny was brown-skinned and had a head full of gray hair. She was a bit heavyset, with one arm a little bigger than the other due to her lymphedema. She was from Spartanburg, South Carolina, and despite having lived in Jersey more than thirty-five years, she still had a very Southern accent.

My family provided the kind of upbringing and support system anyone would hope their children would have. The type of care, wealth, and love that should prevent a child from ever having to experience trauma or the same struggles that affected previous generations. Unfortunately, my life story is proof that no amount of money, love, or support can protect you from a society intent on killing you for your Blackness. Any community that has been taught that anyone not "straight" is dangerous, is in itself a danger to LGBTQIAP+ people.

The elementary school allowed me to start kindergarten at age four because of a loophole in the system and my birthday being a month after school started. I remember having to "test in" to kindergarten because of it. So I was five when this event took place (in the spring of that next year).

By that age I already knew I was different, even though I didn't have the language to explain it or maturity to understand fully what "different" meant. I wasn't gravitating toward typical boy things, like sports, trucks, and so on. I liked baby dolls and doing hair. I could sense that the feelings I had inside of me weren't "right" by society's standards either. I remember that on Valentine's Day, the boys were supposed to give their "crush" a card. Not wanting to give mine to a boy, I gave it to a girl who was clearly a tomboy even at that age. I was always attracted to the company of boys.

I used to daydream a lot as a little boy. But in my daydreams, I was always a girl. I would daydream about having long hair and wearing dresses. And looking back, it wasn't because I thought I was in the wrong body, but because of how I acted more girly. I thought a girl was the only thing I could be.

I struggled with being unable to express myself in my fullest identity. One that would encompass all the things that I liked while still existing in the body of a boy. However, I was old enough to know that I would find safety only in the arms of suppression—hiding my true self—because let's face it, kids can be cruel. I integrated well, though, or so I believed at the time. I became a world-class actor by the age of five, able to blend in with the boys and girls without a person ever questioning my effeminate nature. Then again, we were so little—maybe all the children were just as naïve as I was about the kids who surrounded them.

I was five years old when my teeth were kicked out. It was my introduction to trauma, and now, I'm ready to start there.

At that age, I wasn't allowed to walk home from school by myself. So, I walked home with my older cousins, Little Rall and Rasul. During that time, my cousins lived with our grandmother, who also happened to be our primary caregiver—since our parents worked long hours. Walking to Nanny's house after school was our routine. I usually walked holding hands with Little Rall while Rasul went ahead. We would take the back way every day, which meant walking behind the school, through the football and baseball fields, to the street one block over from Nanny's house. On a normal day, that walk took less than ten minutes. Living so close to the school, I'm sure Nanny never imagined that within those ten minutes, her grandchild's life would be forever scarred.

The memory is vivid. I can still smell the air from that day, sunny and mild springlike weather. That walk to my grandmother's started just like any other, with me holding hands with Rall, while Rasul sped ahead of us. We were at the corner of Lansdowne and Marshall on the lawn of the corner house when we ran into a group of kids from the neighborhood that I didn't recognize.

They had to be about my cousins' ages—around nine or ten years old. The main kid was white. To this day when we talk about it, we use his full name, but I won't say it here. The other kids were Black and white if memory serves me correctly. My cousins knew who they were, I guessed, because they immediately began arguing. When I sit with this memory, there is no sound in the moment. I can see it. When I write about it now, my body can feel it. But as I close my eyes to think about it, the situation was instant chaos. I got extremely nervous. I just held on to Rall's hand even tighter.

There were three of us and six of them, which was really two on six because what did a five-year-old know about fighting? The arguing kept getting more intense with my fear growing as the boys got closer, in each other's faces. It's strange how near to home and safety one can be when some of the most traumatic things in life occur. I used to wonder what would've happened if we had walked a different route that day, or left the school five minutes earlier? Would my life have turned out any different?

Before I knew it, the argument broke into a fight, and I, the invisible boy, somehow became the biggest target. As my cousins squared up with three of the boys, two others grabbed me by my arms and held me on the ground. I screamed for help, as it was all I could do. The third kid swung his leg and kicked me in the face. Then he pulled his leg back again and kicked even harder.

My teeth shattered like glass hitting the concrete. In that moment, I felt nothing. It was as if it were all a dream. Then I felt the pain. I also felt an emotion I had never experienced before: rage. I didn't fully understand the feeling at the time—had not yet had the pleasure of introducing myself to it. The tears that streamed down my face were no longer about pain. I was now crying tears of anger. Tears of rage.

That rage was enough to stop the boy from ever bringing a third kick to my mouth. I somehow broke free, lunged forward, and bit his leg with the teeth I had remaining. He screamed so loud as I bit through his jeans. By this time, my cousins had handled the other three boys and saw what had happened to me. They ran toward us together, which made all my assaulters retreat. They grabbed my book bag, and said, "Run to the house, Matt."

So, I did. Ironically, this moment marked the beginning of my track career, which I would pursue from elementary to high school. Sound is now back on in the memory at this point. I can hear my crying as I ran home. I got to my grandmother's house, and I continued to cry—bloody mouth, busted lip, and baby teeth knocked out.

"What happened?" yelled Nanny.

"We got jumped," my cousins explained. Nanny went and got ice and wrapped it in a paper towel, and she told me to hold it to my face.

It all gets a little hazy after that, as I remember bits and pieces of what occurred. My mother left work immediately to get to Nanny's. She sent an officer ahead to meet us at the house to take down the report. When my mother got there, she came and checked on me immediately. She sat in one of the dining room chairs and had me sit in her lap with her arms around me.

I finally calmed down once my mother held me. At

some point, my uncles showed up and were sitting with us all. My cousins were still visibly upset. I sat there in silence, feeling the rise and fall of my mother's chest with each breath she took. The officer began asking my cousins what happened, and they told their story. The officer asked me to open my mouth so he could note the damage in his report. I recall not speaking for hours after this happened.

When I close my eyes now, I see it all happening as if it were some out-of-body experience. I think back on that day a lot. I wish I knew what motivated the attack. Could it have been because I was effeminate? Could it have been a race thing, since the main assaulter was a white boy from a different part of the neighborhood? Could it have simply been the toxic behaviors we teach boys about fighting and earning manhood? I know that impact and intent always play a role, so even if their intent wasn't those things, the impact would forever change me anyway.

There were no counselors or therapy sessions to help me work through what had happened. Therapy is still very much a taboo subject in the Black community. Those who are seen as having issues with their mental health face a lot of stigma and discrimination because mental health is often conflated with mental illness. So rather than having their child labeled as something hurtful, my parents did the best they could with what they knew.

We did what we always did as a family—we loved on each other even harder. In that moment, my mother just held me, and we sat there together for a long while. Eventually, she took me home. But the next day became just that. The next day. What happened the day before was to be forgotten, or better yet, buried.

Unfortunately, part of what I forgot was how to smile. I immediately became self-conscious about smiling. It's something I've struggled to remedy even as an adult. Because my baby teeth had been kicked out, my adult teeth—almost "buck teeth"—grew in extremely early. Adult-size teeth on a seven-year-old are very odd-looking, and it brought me a whole new type of attention I wasn't looking for. My lips became protection for the smile that was stolen. Picture after picture after picture, I refused to smile. There are photos of me at seven, nine, thirteen, twenty-two, and twenty-nine years old where I refuse to smile.

Every now and again, my mom will find a picture of me with my teeth showing. There aren't many of them, though. And when I look at them, sometimes I cringe. Other times, I've actually teared up, wondering if I was truly happy in that picture or if I simply felt the need to smile because someone said, "Smile, Matt" and I obliged. The fact that I don't feel happy when I look at those images lets me know there wasn't any happiness when I took them.

What did I look like to others—a child who rarely smiled? Did they ever take it as a sign that I was actually dealing with a trauma I couldn't get past? Or did they pass it off as a "boys will be boys" thing that I would eventually grow out of? To go years without smiling in pictures, rarely being questioned why, leaves me to wonder how many signs of trauma we miss or ignore in Black children.

Black boys are required to be rough and tough. To suck up the pain, and not shed a tear. *If you get into a fight, you better win the fight or I'm a beat your ass when you get home* is a phrase I've heard too many times from friends and family throughout my life. Being Black and queer brings on layers of issues.

There can be both a fear of your own community and a fear of dealing with bullying from other children who don't respect your identity. When that kind of pressure builds within a young queer kid, the fear becomes constricting and can wrap you up in layers, each more difficult to peel away as you grow up.

As an adult, I have gone through the unlearning to understand that my community's treatment of Black queer children is in fact a by-product of a system of assimilation to whiteness and respectability that forces Black people to fit one mold in society, one where being a man means you must be straight and masculine. I didn't have the ability to separate my Blackness from my queerness. The loss of my smile was as much a denial of my Black joy as it was my queer joy. When I did smile, it was a coping mechanism. My smile was a mask that hid the pain of suppressing who I was.

Masking is a common coping mechanism for a Black queer boy. We bury the things that have happened to us, hoping that they don't present themselves later in our adult life. Some of us never realize that subconsciously, these buried bones are what dictate our every navigation and interaction throughout life.

Oddly enough, many of us connect with each other through trauma and pain: broken people finding other broken people in the hopes of fixing one another.

I used to think that I had gotten over it if I took a good picture where I was smiling. But it only required one bad smiling pic to remind me of how trauma has a funny way of showing up in our lives during the moments when we least expect it. It can be an action that we write off as something else, when really it is the manifestation of a pain we had refused to deal with. A trauma that no one helped us fully process or that they didn't have the skills to even know we needed help for. *Boys aren't supposed to cry, so hold that shit in.* Sometimes to the grave.

There have been times when I brushed my teeth too hard and got a taste of blood and was immediately taken back to that day. An adult, crying in a bathroom mirror, pretending I didn't know why.

Trauma appears all throughout pop culture, often sung by the masses as a hot lyric, penned by the performer as a release of that pain. The trauma is shared by the community, too. Songs become our battle cries; trauma becomes the thing that bonds us together. So much so, that I've heard people actually say, "I need sad Mary J. Blige to come back because her music is better." Our community struggles to connect with joy in the way that we have with pain.

When I hear Cardi B say, she "gotta bag and fixed [her] teeth," it's more than a cute line in a dope song. And yes, "Bodak Yellow" was a bop! But she is responding to years of hate and flack she received for having crooked teeth. She is talking about the trauma she dealt with, and what she was able to do to gain back agency over those moments, and then use it in a way to make folks proud. Every time she speaks about her teeth, she is allowing herself to work through the process of healing rather than be burdened by the weight of holding the trauma in.

For years, I held that traumatic moment inside of me, and it was reflected in hundreds of pictures that captured my face absent a smile. I tried smiling with my mouth closed or making faces. As I got older, I would get hit on by guys and crack a smile. They would say, "You have a nice smile" and my instant reaction was to roll my eyes in disbelief. And I'd even have friends send me messages saying, "I noticed you don't ever smile." I would deflect the comments and give some reason that had nothing to do with what

I was actually feeling. I still had that five-year-old in me who was not ready to smile. This queer in me that couldn't fully be.

January 15, 2015, would signal a change in my smile-related trauma. My mother had two brain aneurysms that day. It was a dire situation, and my family was very unprepared. As a thirty-year-old, I knew I had to hold it all together. I was her eldest and I knew she would need me.

I remember the doctor saying, "It's time to take her back to the prep room. Two people can come to walk her in." My father and I decided that it would be us. They wheeled her into the prep room right before you go into the OR and told us, "You have one minute." My dad stood on one side of her bed, and I stood on the other. He leaned in and gave her a kiss, and she said, "I'm going to be fine."

I stood there. Nervous. *Terrified.* I finally gave her a kiss, too. As I pulled away, she could see that I was choking up. In that moment, I felt like that five-year-old boy sitting on his mother's lap just after losing his teeth. And she, in her moment of need, was my comfort. It was as if she always knew that I hadn't gotten past that day. And before she went into that operating room, she needed to make sure that I did. As a tear rolled from each of my eyes, she looked up at me and said: "Smile, Matt. Just smile."

I gave her the biggest smile I ever had since the day I lost it.

My mom survived her surgery, and I learned a valuable lesson about holding on to trauma. It's necessary that we do the work to unpack our shit. It's time for the world to let queer Black boys unpack their shit.

Smile, Black boys.

PS: The day after my teeth were kicked out, my cousins went back up to our school with my uncle and beat up the main boy and his father while waiting for school to start. They got suspended for five days. Don't mess with family.

CHAPTER 2

IDENTITY

"Matthew . . . MATTHEW!!!" Nanny was yelling for me.

"What?"

"Don't you *what* me, boy."

I ran downstairs and stood in front of the big chair in the living room where Nanny sat and said, "Yes, Nanny?"

"Go upstairs and grab my purse from behind the door."

"Okay," I said, and again I went running. I was

always Nanny's go-for to retrieve something. You know, *go-for this* or *go-for that*. I actually enjoyed being her helper, though. She would often make you come from upstairs to where she was downstairs only to send you back upstairs to where you'd just left, to get what she needed, and come back to her. Nanny was old school. She liked to make sure she saw you before giving you instructions.

The towering yellow house on Lansdowne Terrace in Plainfield was my second home. We used to call it the "Big House," in comparison to my parents' home, which was much smaller. This was Nanny's house and our daily refuge after a long, rigorous day of elementary school. With my parents working, my brother and I would stay there after school every day from about 3 p.m. to 9 p.m. My mom would then come and pick us up after her time at the salon and bring us home.

The Big House was always fun because my cousins Rall and Rasul lived there, as well as my aunt Munch (when not in college). When I was a kid, Nanny's house also felt like "home." There were plenty of times Friday would come, and my mother would ask if we wanted to come home or stay the weekend. My younger brother and I *always* opted to stay for the weekend—which I'm sure our mother appreciated since she also worked at her salon on Saturdays.

The Big House also meant family. There was a big dining room table there, and Nanny loved cooking on Sundays and having all the Elders—Mom and Nanny's side of the family—over for dinner to watch football on the big-screen TV in the living room.

I recall one particular Sunday evening though when me and my cousin Little Rall were teasing each other—playfully—like we always did. The jokes started off very mild.

"That's why you short," I remember saying to him.

"That's why you ugly," he said back.

Everyone was letting it happen because it seemed harmless enough at first; no one would get their feelings hurt. But that all changed very quickly when I made a joke about his grades. For reference, I was a straight-A student—considered a nerd by most standards. My cousins knew that I was smart, and they weren't as much jealous about it as they were irritated. See, I was always used as the gold standard for how everyone else's grades should have been. So I said it:

"That's why you get bad grades."

This pissed him all the way off. Luckily for me, Little Rall was always my protector so I didn't worry much about him ever retaliating violently. Had this been Rasul, the result would've been different for sure. But Little Rall, instead of hitting me physically, went below the belt and hit me in the worst way possible. With a truth that most in my family were not ready for me to learn, whatever their reasons:

"THAT'S WHY YOUR REAL NAME IS GEORGE."

I stood there shocked at the statement. First, because I thought, *What a stupid comeback*. Second, because I just knew that it wasn't true. So, I said to him, "No, it's not!" To which he responded, "Yes, it is. Your name is George not Matthew." This time, I got upset and started yelling, "My name is not George, my name is Matthew!" repeatedly until Nanny walked from the kitchen into the dining room, where we were arguing.

"What is all this noise?"

I looked at her and said, "Little Rall keeps saying my name is George, that my name isn't Matthew." Her face became stone solid, teeth clenched. She looked at Little Rall with that face that every Black child fears from a Black mother. That face where you could see the words in their eyes before they spoke them: "I'm gonna beat your ass when everyone goes home." Luckily for Little Rall, she could see how upset I was and opted to deal with him later.

"Come into the living room, Matt, and let's talk."

I sat on the couch with Nanny and she explained that Little Rall was correct, that my real name was George. I just remember sitting there and pondering what that meant. Like, did that mean I was supposed to be a different person? Was some mistake made when I was born? Did everyone else in the family go by fake names, too?

I was devastated by the news. It felt like my whole reality had been shattered, and I could not process what it all meant. I asked a bunch of questions, starting with, "Why don't y'all use my real name?"

Pull up your seats, everyone, because it's story time. Stories are a common theme in this book, so you might wanna get some popcorn, too. Although I wasn't told at the time why my family decided to not use my given name, they felt more comfortable sharing the story once I got older.

Let's go back to the hospital room where I was born . . .

My parents and grandmother were gathered around as they made the decision about what I would be named. At the time, my father was insistent upon all his sons' names starting with a *G*. My older brother was already a junior—named Gregory Girard Johnson Jr., after my dad. So, my dad, in all his creativity, thought my name should be Girard Gregory Johnson. Did I mention my father was country? You'll understand why later. Thankfully, my mother and Nanny gave him an emphatic "try again."

So then my father decided that I would follow in the line of *his* father and brother and be named "George." My grandfather's name was George Washington Johnson. It's okay to laugh, as I did when I first heard it as a child. And my father's brother was named George Stevenson Johnson. And it's okay to laugh at his name, too. The second attempt at my name was to make me a junior under his brother—George Stevenson Johnson Jr.—since my uncle had three daughters. To this idea, my mother and Nanny gave him another "try again." Anyone who knows my father knows he is the king of his castle and wants things his way. So, when it was all said and done, they compromised: He could pick my first name as long as Nanny and my mother could pick the middle one.

It was in that moment that Nanny pulled out her Bible and told my mother, "This baby is going to have a biblical middle name, because there is no way in hell that I am calling a little baby George." As they thumbed through the chapters, "Matthew" struck a chord with them. He was a good character from the Bible, in their opinion, and they felt that I looked like a Matthew. On that day, George Matthew Johnson entered the world, but Matthew Johnson left that hospital.

Jumping back to that night in the Big House: Nanny felt I was too young to hear that story, knowing it would've only led to me asking more questions, so she gave me a generic answer, "We just decided to go with your middle name."

That night, my mom came to pick me and my brother up, and my grandmother told her what had happened. Mom asked if I was okay, and I told her, "Yeah, I'm fine." But honestly, I wasn't. She thought nothing more of it and drove us back home. Little did she know that this issue was far from over for me.

The next day, I went to school and everything seemed normal. Mrs. P. called out the attendance like she did every day—going down the list of names to see who was absent on her roster. "Matthew Johnson" she said aloud, to which I responded, "Here." Class went on as it usually did that day. We had a quiz, and she gave us thirty minutes to complete it.

"Pencils down everyone," Mrs. P. called as the timer rang.

When she got to my desk, I handed her my paper. She glanced at it, then looked at me, and down at the paper again. It seemed as if she knew something was going on but wasn't sure if it was one of those things that should be addressed in front of the class or in private. She said nothing at the time and moved on to correcting papers. Throughout the day she gave out other assignments for the English and science portions of class. Each time she gave us another paper, I did my work and then wrote my name on top:

George Johnson

It never even crossed my mind that the teacher might be concerned that I was having an identity crisis. As a kid, I adapted very quickly to change, much better than I ever have as an adult. I was able to shift from the night before, where I felt my whole life had been a lie, to the next day, where I thought it was cool that I had a different name. This ease showcased my ability to just go with the flow. I had agency—the power to control my narrative—and this was a moment where I was choosing to do what I felt was best for me, no questions asked. As a child who so rarely got to choose his path, in a society that expected me to check off a particular box about my identity, this was one choice I was able to make. One identity marker that I had the power to define.

I was excited to write my name every chance I got that day. I kept going back and forth with the way I would make my G's. I was in my own little world, telling all my friends that my real name was George. To an eight-year-old, this was headline news. Their friend whose name was Matthew just yesterday was now going by George! The event caused a bit of a ruckus, because of course other kids wanted to change their names, too. I kept telling them they would have to check with their parents first to get permission, as I did.

After school, we walked to Nanny's house as usual, sat at the table, and began doing our homework. As soon as we wrapped that up, we went upstairs to my cousins' room and began playing video games. We could hear the phone ringing, but we hardly ever got any phone calls, so we rarely answered—unless Nanny shouted, "Get the damn phone." This time, she didn't, and I heard Nanny answer it herself in her usual white-lady voice, saying, "Hellooo." After a minute or two, she yelled for me.

"MATT!!! Come down here and get the phone. It's your mommy."

I came running into the foyer area, where Nanny was standing. "Here, baby." She passed the phone over.

"Hey, Matt. I want to talk about what name you want to use," my mother said. "The teacher called home today and was concerned about you changing your name on all of your papers to George."

I remember telling her, "Yeah, I wrote it since it's my real name."

"I know, but now you have a decision to make. You can either go by George or you can go by Matthew. You can take some time to decide. But you can't go back and forth, so we gotta choose one." In that moment, I got a little nervous. Nervous that I would disappoint them by going with George over Matthew.

Before I could say anything else, she said, "No one will be mad at you for changing it. You are old enough to make this decision on your own."

My mother always knew just what to say to me. She knew how important it was for me, even at the age of eight, to be making this decision for myself. One that I didn't have a choice in originally. I paused for a few seconds to think about it. Nanny was still standing there, waiting for me to decide. Then I said, "I'm gonna keep Matthew."

"Okay . . . Matthew it is. I'll let your teacher know. I'll see you later, okay?"

"Okay, Mommy!"

And just like that, my name was back to Matthew.

I was able to use the name Matthew all the way up through middle school—which happened to be in the public school system. In public school, they allowed me to go by my middle name on all the rosters. By the time I got to ninth grade however, Matthew was a no-go for the strict standards of my Catholic school.

"George Johnson" was the legal name on the attendance roll that first day of ninth grade, and no, they were not willing to change that to Matthew Johnson.

There were a few kids in the Catholic school that had gone to elementary and middle school with me. As soon as they heard the name and me say "Here," they looked at me like, "Who the f*** is George?" That first week, I remember saying, "Yes, that's my real name" over and over again. Funny enough, my entire family was also still not going for it. So in school I was called George all day, only to get home and be Matthew to my family, friends, and anyone else who had known me growing up.

My name has been George to some and Matthew to others since that time. And although I think this is a funnier story in the lexicon of what has been my interesting life, I feel there is a deeper meaning here. This story isn't about my name. It isn't about the shock of the eight-year-old who felt some cruel trick was being played on him, or the thirteen-year-old who would have to accept using his first name.

This is about identity. This is about culture and how it dictates what is a "good" and "bad" name, especially in the Black community. This is about the politics around sex and gender, and that when our parents choose a name that we as children are uncomfortable with, we have the right to change it.

My mother respected my agency by allowing me to choose what would work best for me. But would that conversation have been so simple if I'd wanted my name to be Dominique or Samantha? Even as a child, there was an understanding that the name I went by was meant for the comfort of my family. That yes, even though they didn't want to call a baby George, at some point it would no longer be their decision to make. My name was meant for me, and me alone.

Going to a Catholic school that didn't allow me to use a "preferred name" also taught me a valuable lesson in conformity. In addition to having students wear the same uniforms, the school expected us to uphold a set of social and behavioral standards. We were all forced to attend Mass and take a religion class, despite what our own religious beliefs may have been. And we were disciplined for anything that questioned or didn't fit within any of these standards. As restrictive as these standards were, they prepared me for when I entered spaces later in life that required me to meet respectability standards in order to be accepted. These conformist structures did force me to act out in other ways while in school.

In one specific instance, I wore a basketball headband on a dress-down day. I had made it through three periods before a teacher told me I had to take it off, which I refused to do. She repeated, "You are not allowed to wear that headband in my class."

"Well, I'm not taking it off, so what is the next step?" I said.

In a very smug voice, she said, "I'm writing you up and assigning you detention."

"Okay, but this headband is staying on."

Agency—a word I didn't know when I was that young—is a guiding principle that I wish we taught young kids about more. Rather than saying, "You are wearing this," I hope more adults will ask, "What would you like to wear?" And then have a conversation about those choices. When we see our children not conforming to the societal standards of heterosexuality or we see them gravitating to things of the "opposite gender," I would love for us to ask the deeper questions about who and what they are.

Your name is one of the most important pieces of your identity. It is the thing that you own. It is attached to every piece of work that you put into the world. Your name holds power when you walk into a room. No two people with the same name are the same person. It's important that, like everything else you grow to love in life, your name is something you appreciate as well.

Should you not like your name, change it. It is yours, and it will stay with you forever, so do with it what you wish. As we continue to grow through sex and gender, many people will take back their power and change their names—choosing one that fits the person they are, not the one society pushed them to be. Keep your name if you like it. But know that you don't have to.

The most important thing to realize is that you have the agency to make decisions that are in your best interest. The power to push back against society and even those in your own home. It is unfortunate that we live in a world where owning your agency could be met with rejection, disrespect, or even violence—especially for those owning their queer identity from a young age.

Suffice it to say, respect people for their names, and for how they choose to identify. This also goes for respecting people and their choice of pronouns—he/him, she/her, they/them, god, goddess, or whatever. We are conditioned to think these things should be the exception. People being allowed to be called by their chosen names and their gender pronouns *is the rule*.

Let yourself unlearn everything you thought you knew about yourself, and listen to what you need to know about those who navigate life outside the margins of a heterosexual box. I bet most of you never thought to ever question if you even like your name. Or question if that was something you had the power to change if you didn't. I hope you will now . . .

CHAPTER 3

"HONEYCHILD"

We lived in a ranch-style house, where all the rooms were on the same floor. My brother and I shared the same room, which was next to my parents' and sat at the end of a hallway. The third bedroom in our house was used as a guest room in case anyone should come to visit. When it wasn't full, we used it as another place for storage. My father is what many would call a "pack rat"—meaning he throws nothing away. Unless he bought something new to replace something, and even then, he would much rather keep the old

one "just in case." Most of the toys from my childhood are still in the house, with my father's explana-
tion that "they might be worth something one day."

In our room, we had two wooden bunk beds—half
the year stacked on top of each other, the other half of
the year split apart on opposite sides of the room, just
as we liked it. There was one closet that stored our
toys and most of my grandmother's clothing—the one
who lived in Virginia—from the past thirty years. Like
I said, my father never throws anything away.

We each had a dresser, mine tall and narrow and
my brother's long and wide, but we shared everything
else in the room, including the television. We got along
for the most part, so we never had any arguments over
what to watch. We were both getting ready for bed
one evening when my mother called to me from the
living room.

She was sitting there, waiting for me on the couch,
watching TV. We had a television in every room. Another thing my father just couldn't go without. As I
walked up to her, she said, "Sit down, Matt. I gotta
talk to you about something."

That "something" had apparently been building
up in school for several weeks without me knowing.

She then went on to ask, "So, what is this word you have been using in class to talk to other kids?"

Here's some background info.

I was *very* sassy as a little kid. A *sissy* is what the kids used to call me back then, before they got older and escalated to the word *faggot*. I remember I used to watch the way women would walk with a switch—that movement of the hips, going side to side as you walk forward. I had a natural switch, but I knew I wasn't supposed to walk like that, so I tried my best not to—emphasis on *tried*.

I was skinny and for sure didn't have any hips. But back then, before other kids got cruel, I would try my best to throw my little body from side to side when I walked—even more than my natural walk was already doing. My family always said, "Stop switching, Matt!" But I would just laugh, even when someone told me to stop doing it and go back to walking "like a boy."

I was still in the second grade—a happy kid, a little talkative, but overall a good kid. I was considered smart, based on all the standardized tests they would make us take. I always enjoyed getting my scores back and seeing I was "above the national average."

As far as my social life was concerned, I was mainly friends with girls. I gravitated toward them because they were a reflection of what I was feeling on the inside. I would kind of act like them, perform some of their mannerisms—or at least that's what I thought to myself. I was too young to ask myself whether my performance was innate or not—although I know now that I wasn't imitating anyone. The bent wrists, the walk, the sassiness was a reflection of my own image.

I want to stay with that thought for a second. There are moments even now when I'm simply not sure of my mannerisms, femininity, and more. Are they derived from mirroring the Black women in my life, or are they naturally me, or a mix of both? I know that it doesn't matter. And that regardless of how my mannerisms come across, they are natural to me. I just like to think about all the ways I came to be me.

My friends and I would use words and phrases like *hey, girl* and *chiiilld*, which only grown folks were supposed to use, but we were kids pretending we were grown. As long as we were out of earshot of any adults, we figured we could get away with it. One of my friends at school was a tall white girl, a little plain but very friendly. I loved her last name, as weird as that may sound. It was "Haudenschild." I used to wish that I had a cool last name like that.

It was around this same time that I also met someone new in my personal life. I say that as if I had a personal life as an eight-year-old, but there was a new adult coming around the family. She was dating my uncle Rall. Crystal was one of the prettiest, coolest, and wittiest Black women I had ever met. She always had her fingernails done and would wear her hair with blond and red highlights. I used to think she looked like the singer Faith Evans. She also drove a white Cadillac.

She was always fun to be around and would take me and my cousins out as she was getting to know the family. I called her Ms. Crystal at the time, although she would later become Aunt Crystal. To my uncle Rall and others, she was known by her nickname, "Honey." Honey was so fitting a name for a person who was so cool. I would secretly think about what it would feel like if my name were Honey, too. Of course, the whole time I was daydreaming, I was also envisioning myself as a girl and sometimes a woman.

I rarely, if ever, imagined myself in daydreams as a boy growing older. In my daydreams, I got to live as who I *felt* I was. I saw myself as a girl or woman that looked like my mom—especially because we look alike. My mannerisms were that of her and other women I grew up with, primarily my aunts.

But in reality, I was still a boy. Although I didn't have the power to live as I was in my daydreams, I did have to make the best of my current situation. I wanted to feel more like one of the girls, but I knew that I wasn't going to be able to use "girl lingo" without other kids looking at me different. Boys were supposed to speak one way. And girls were supposed to speak another. So, I would do my best to not use girl lingo when I was around boys, and vice versa. I was "code-switching" long before I knew what code-switching was.

One day, me and a group of girls were talking—more like gossiping—when instead of just saying "girl!" or "child," I said, "*Honey*child . . ." The word just rolled off my tongue so naturally, full of sass. The girls looked stunned, and I knew why. I grinned, bent my little wrist in their direction, said "Honeychild" again, and continued the rest of my sentence. Then one of them did the same and followed my lead. I had created my first term in gay lingo, even though I didn't know what being gay was.

It wasn't until I was much older that I learned about "gay lingo." Terms like *shade* and *yaaassss* that we so often hear used in television or on social media—especially by those *not* from the LGBTQIAP+ community—have become common in pop culture. Lingo that children like me were ostracized for using. Lingo that queer children today *still* get ostracized for using. And yet straight people use it out of context safely.

This lingo or slang was created by "Black femmes," which is an umbrella term that captures Black trans women, Black queer men, nonbinary folk, cishet Black women, and anyone else I may be missing. However, a lot of this history has been erased from those who identify as queer, which has allowed the notion that queer culture comes from emulating Black cishet women to spread. But it's not true. That erasure also allows the hetero community to get "a pass" for using language that would often get queer folk harmed.

On that day, the three of us including Haudens-child started using the word. It was so fun to have some lingo that I could call my own. It made me feel like the women in my mother's salon who used to gossip. I felt powerful and free.

For the next few weeks in school, we used "Honeychild" in conversations we were having together, and also apart. Although I was primarily using the word only with people I felt comfortable with, the other girls were using it with everyone. Before long, the entire class knew of the word "Honeychild," boys included. The word that was once shared lingo between friends quickly became a classroom term. The word then escaped the confines of our little classroom and spread all the way to kids' homes.

Adults began to wonder why a boy would be saying a term so "feminine." Unfortunately, the creativity of children often comes under fire when it doesn't meet the acceptable standard of gender performance. Meaning, had a girl created this term, it likely wouldn't have caused as much of a fuss with anyone. But the fact that "Honeychild" was created by a boy elicited grave concerns.

I'll be honest in this moment. I can only assume that my classmates' parents took issue with using the word. It wasn't as if they spoke directly to me about it, or my parents. But I've lived long enough to know that today's adults are still uncomfortable with boys who do anything not considered "masculine."

One of the parents complained to our teacher about their child using the word and who it originated from. My teacher worried about the greater good of the students, and then took it upon herself to call my mother and ask if she could have a talk with me about no longer using the word.

I sat next to my mother on the couch that evening. "Mrs. P. said that you created a word called 'Honey-child.' What's it mean?"

So, I told her that I used it to refer to boys and girls instead of saying their name.

"Well, they are saying that other kids are using the word and that it's become a class distraction, so you have to stop saying it."

When you are a child that is different, there always seems to be a "something." You can't switch, you can't say *that*, you can't act this way. There is always a *something* that must be erased—and with it, a piece of you. The fear of being that vulnerable again outweighs the happiness that comes with being who you are, and so you agree to erase that something.

Language is interesting, especially as a child. Kids have been known to create their own words and languages that they can share amongst themselves—often looked at as harmless. Yet in this case, my invented language was seen as a threat to masculinity—an ideal I was supposed to be living up to even though I wasn't old enough to fully understand its meaning or, for that matter, even how to spell it.

So the adults in my life dictated what masculinity would look like for me. It was also their responsibility to ensure that the person I was, this "sissy," didn't influence other children—as if my being who I was would change who others were. But that's how they thought. My word was a threat to the identity of their kids—the identity they hoped their kids would have.

Nowadays, when I think of the word "Honeychild," I get to sit back and giggle. Giggle at the fact that it was once a threat, but is now as common as putting on your socks every day. Like I stated earlier, gay lingo dominates language in this society now. I have watched the language once weaponized against me now being commercialized for millions to use, see, and enjoy.

Except for Black queer people. Our use of the language that we created out of exclusion is still being used against us—as it was when I was a child. Our use of it makes us easier targets. We aren't allowed to live as we are in the culture that we continue to shape and create. We get to watch those who oppress us use our content with none of the repercussions we face.

I remember not feeling upset about "Honeychild," but also not really understanding it either. I just said, "Okay, Mommy," and she smiled. I went back to my room and finished getting ready for bed. I never used the word again—but now I know the trauma that had been triggered because I have never forgotten the word. Like I never forgot the way I learned my given name. Like I never forgot being jumped as a little boy in kindergarten. I just put it away somewhere in my mind, hoping it would never resurface.

That would be the last time I created any lingo for myself. I didn't really shut down, but I knew it must've had something to do with me being girly. It seemed the only time I was told I couldn't do something or was chastised for it was when I was being too feminine.

Children remember. As much as we hold on to the good moments, we also keep the bad ones. Children are also burdened with the stresses their parents face as they attempt to guide their kids to meet a societal standard. My parents shared this fear and with valid reason. As much as they likely wanted to fight for me to be able to live "as I was," they also knew the dangers my sassiness could place me in.

Thankfully, they parented with my best interests in mind instead of their potential embarrassment for raising a child like me. At times, they parented out of fear, knowing they couldn't protect me when I left the house. Likely, there was a mixture of it all. But they never attempted to "beat the gay out of me," although they knew I was gay from a very young age. They did the best they could with the knowledge they had at the time.

But later that night, I realized the only place that was truly safe for me would be in my imagination. My ability to be a kid came at the expense of my gender identity. The suppression continued that day. The moments that I wanted to cry would be covered up with laughter. A fake closed-lip smile would be used to hide the pain I was feeling from my inability to be me. That was the first day I began wearing the mask. The mask that would cover my face, so no one could see who I really was.

CHAPTER 4

FAGS PLAY FOOTBALL, TOO

"Downnnn!" the quarterback would yell. All the boys in my elementary school would get into position. You could hear whoever the quarterback was that day from everywhere on the playground. It was like watching the NFL, but with aggressive ten-year-olds. The QB would look to the left and then to the right. He was checking to make sure his teammates had gotten into their first position.

"Blue 42! . . . Blue 42! . . ."

"Set . . . HIKE!"

Football was the highlight of most boys' days.

Unless you were a boy named Matthew Johnson. I absolutely dreaded the thought of ever having to play football. My male classmates were such . . . boys to me. Like rough, tough, shit-talking boys. And I wasn't. I always saw these kind of boys as a threat. The hyper-assertive, masculine, dominating types. These types of boys made it very clear that I was nothing like them. And when I didn't fear these types of boys at school, I had a constant reminder of them at home.

I didn't have the best relationship with my cousin Rasul, who I often got into fights with at Nanny's house. He was a few years older than me, so I never won any of them. It was definitely one of those "love-hate" relationships. We often talk about bullies in school, but rarely when they are in our own families. He could be my biggest protector and my worst enemy.

By now I was in the fifth grade—old enough to know that football just wasn't my thing. For that and many other reasons . . .

I chose to opt out.

Fortunately, we had several other ways to fill recess, everyone's favorite part of the day. For those who didn't want to participate in football, there was basketball. We had a full-length basketball court on black pavement right by the pond that sat next to our school. It even had a side for the overflow kids who were waiting to get into the next game. The court also sat beside the large field where the other boys would play football. And still . . .

I chose to opt out.

For those of us who didn't want to do either, there was a full playground that sat on top of wooden chips. Our playground had been updated a few years back with all new equipment—a slide, swings, monkey bars, and balance beam. Being kids, we turned this into our own obstacle course, much like the *American Gladiators* television show that was on during that time . . . which most of you probably don't have a clue about. Think, *American Ninja Warrior* but about twenty years ago.

Two people would race to see who could get to the slide first, where they would run up it and then climb down the ladder. Next, you would climb up the monkey bars and swing to get to the other side, where you would then jump down and walk the balance beam. After the balance beam, you would run, weaving through the swings, and cross the finish line. I used to love doing this obstacle course in the third and fourth grades. Then, I was in fifth grade and . . .

I chose to opt out.

Luckily for me, I found a new love during recess. My joy came in the form of two jump ropes being turned simultaneously. One going in a clockwise direction and the other counter to it. The ropes would hit the ground with the beat of a clock—tick, tock, tick, tock, tick, tock, until a person made a mistake hitting the rope or jumped out to give someone else a turn. Double-Dutching became my new daily freedom. It was my escape.

We would jump at the top of the hill that overlooked the playground and all the other kids engaged in the various activities. The hill was directly above the field where most of the boys played football. The first time I went up there, the girls were so eager to teach me. I could already jump using one rope, as we had done it in gym class hundreds of times, but two ropes seemed complicated.

Sure enough, I was terrible at it. To begin with, I was nervous that there was no way I could get in between the two ropes. My brain was analytical and always trying to figure shit out. I couldn't process jumping in between two moving ropes. But I watched the girls jump in with varying speeds and find a way to jump out without being touched by the ropes. I was convinced I was going to do it. And then one day, I did.

I jumped in.

This game connected to my effeminate feelings. Double-Dutching was my little way of getting that out of my system, when I felt I couldn't be "sassy" in front of friends or family. That half hour every day became my solace, and those ropes became more than just a game.

It was me jumping in between personas: the person I wanted to be on the inside versus the person society told me I had to be on the outside. My pride grew with each mistake, each welt from the rope hitting my legs. They were battle scars for the hard effort I was putting in daily to perfect my jump roping abilities.

Around this time, girls started "developing" as my grandmother would say—or, to put it simply, growing breasts. So, they would jump in the ropes and hold down their chests. I would giggle inside because they looked so silly doing it, but it was their way of acknowledging they were growing, truth be told. Some girls were flat chested, holding on to absolutely nothing. I would imitate them. It made me feel more in touch with my femininity, and the girl in my head I always daydreamed about.

I was the *only* boy who double-Dutched, so it was quite clear this was something boys were not supposed to do. Better yet, boys didn't have the space to do this without being ridiculed. Truthfully, jumping rope should've never been a gendered activity to begin with. The girls never seemed to mind me taking part, though.

There was something so perfectly girly about jumping double Dutch—not to mention all of the fun songs you could sing while you were at it. When using only one rope to jump, this was our go-to song:

"Teddy Bear, Teddy Bear,
Turn around!
Teddy Bear, Teddy Bear,
Touch the ground . . ."

Oh, but when we were double-Dutching, we always went to my favorite, because you could almost curse:

"Miss Lucy had a steamboat,
The steamboat had a bell, (Toot! Toot!)

Miss Lucy went to heaven,
And the steamboat went to
Hell-o, operator . . ."

If you could make it through the song, then you got to do Hot Pepper—where both turners would turn as fast as they could until you either jumped out or got hit with the rope. We all used to end up with so many welts on our arms and legs after recess from getting smacked by those ropes. But we had so much fun regardless.

One day, it became painfully obvious that I couldn't juggle the identities anymore. That a boy jumping rope was not meant to be a thing, no matter how innocent. Boys were supposed to like sports and getting dirty. Boys were supposed to be friends with boys and have crushes on girls. They weren't supposed to try to *be* girls. That day came much sooner than I was ready for, and I made a decision that changed my navigation through life forever.

It was a comfortable day in April, and we were nearing the end of the school year. Lunch was always interesting because I would sit with the boys and talk about "boy" things, but then immediately go to recess and get with my girls. Code-switching like that, navigating disparate spaces like that, was pretty much normal.

Unfortunately, this day at recess would be much different. We were all excused from lunch and went out the big double doors to recess. As usual, the kids all went to their designated locations: the football field, the basketball court, the playground with the wooden chips, just like clockwork. Then there was me, minding my own business and going to the top of the hill to get ready for another day of double-Dutching.

We were about to get started when a friend of mine named Todd came to the top of the hill from the football field. He tapped me on the shoulder and asked if he could talk to me for a moment, so he and I walked away from the girls. Todd and I had been friends for several years at this point. We worked on some class projects together, and even had sleepovers. He was a white kid at a predominantly Black school, but he fit in very well. Folks considered him cool, and it was cool that he and I were friends.

He let me know that the other boys had been talking about me. Now, I was used to having the boys talk about me, but I knew it must've been bad for Todd to come and speak to me about it. He told me the other boys were saying that I wanted to be a girl, with several of them calling me a fag. Inside I was hot, not with anger but with fear. I had seen enough arguments, and enough boys who likely weren't gay be called a faggot—and both typically led to fights. When called a faggot, it immediately became a case of fight or flight—but walking away from the altercation was seen as a sign of weakness and admission that you were, in fact, gay.

My problem was that I was being called those slurs while exhibiting effeminate characteristics, and while also doing things that girls traditionally did. So for me, it would have to be about balancing those traditionally feminine qualities and measuring my safety as we got older. I knew the bullying would only get worse if I continued to fall into this effeminate line.

I hated being referred to as a faggot. I had a physical reaction anytime I was called that word. The nerves shot off in my body. I knew that I had been called one before, but never to my face, so I just ignored it. This time, though, I couldn't.

As much as this was about me, it was also about Todd and those who liked to associate with me. "Birds of a feather flock together." So, them calling me names like faggot, meant that those associating with me got caught up in it, too. People who are straight that associate with me now, as an adult, still get questioned about their sexuality. Simply because they are friends with me. Adults who participate in homophobia create kids that do the same.

Homophobia denies queer people happiness. I imagine there are a lot of queer people who would love to play sports or do traditionally "masculine" activities, but they hold themselves back based on the fear of interacting with people they can't trust. People who have made it very clear that queer people are unwelcome despite the fact they have talent. Homophobia is the reason that so many who currently play sports are closeted—as there is no way football, baseball, and basketball are 99.9 percent heterosexual.

We watched Michael Sam become one of the best college athletes in the game only to be demonized for his sexuality. Dominant culture's inability to integrate his queerness into a masculine-centered sport like football stole the opportunity of a lifetime from him. It wasn't that he didn't have the talent. Sometimes you just don't have the strength to carry the burden and do the job. Navigating in a space that questions your humanity isn't really living at all. It's existing. We all deserve more than just the ability to exist.

Todd had an idea for how we could fix our situation. "You should play football with us today. Even if it's just for one day, it will get them to stop talking about you." I wish I could say I'd had a thought in my head other than *Do what you have to do to make you feel okay.* For me, being "okay" just meant not being talked about. I remember looking at the girls and telling them I wasn't going to be jumping with them that day.

Opting out chose me.

We walked back down the hill together to the field, where about fifteen boys stood ready to get the game started. I knew who all the boys were—I was friends with some—but not enough to make me feel comfortable. I remember being asked, "Have you ever even played football?"

"Yeah, with my cousins," I said. The moment was tense. It wasn't lost on me that I was now looking for acceptance from the same boys who denied me the agency to do the things I preferred, like double-Dutching.

But I struggled with not being liked. I was also a skinny kid and didn't have my cousins around to fight this battle, as they had moved on to middle school. This was a choice I was making to ensure that I was able to get through my days. Even if it meant I was pushing away the things I loved. It was worth it for the momentary feeling of being liked.

Oddly enough, I *did* play sports on weekends. My cousins would come to this same playground area and teach me how to play basketball, baseball, and most importantly, how to catch a football. I did those things with my cousins because it was fun, and I enjoyed them—never out of pressure.

This circumstance was about my need for survival. We got out there and I was on offense with about seven other boys. The quarterback drew the play on the football, and we all broke from the huddle.

"Downnnn!"

He looked to the left. Then he looked to the right.

"Blue 42! . . . Blue 42! . . ."

"Set . . . HIKE!"

I shot out of the formation like a rocket on a slant pattern—that is, running up five steps and then cutting out toward the sidelines. The ball was thrown for me, and I caught it. What happened next though is still a mystery to me.

The first boy came up to tackle me, but I didn't go down. Then came a second and then a third. Before you knew it, I had three of them trying to take me, but I just wouldn't go down. I dragged them all the way into the end zone that day. I didn't care how heavy they were; there was a spirit in me that was going to prove I was just as tough as they were—and better at their sports. The other kids were watching in shock, and then excitement.

My team ran up to me and we celebrated really quick. High fives and daps all around before it was time for the other team to get the ball back. Everyone mentioned how "tough" I was. For me, it was one of the greatest days of my elementary-school life. It was a moment that helped me to understand that not only was I actually very good at sports, but I could also use my talent as a shield from bullying.

Football and basketball became my new thing. Although I eventually learned to like playing those sports, I felt a deep sadness the day I stopped jumping rope. It was the moment I realized that safety trumped satisfaction, even as a kid. I would often look back to the top of the hill, even as I did my best to fit in with the rest of the boys on the fields down below.

It was interesting to finally feel like I was one of the boys. Hearing the conversations they had about girls, the cursing, and the tough-guy act. They talked about sex, although none had actually had it. Up until this point, I'd had a few friends that were boys, but those friendships were mainly based on the fact that I had good grades and was kinda funny with the shade (before "shade" was actually a thing). Now I had a reason for the boys to really like me.

I was never picked first at recess, but I was also never picked last. That meant something to me. It meant that folks were looking past my femininity, which was a relief, even if for a moment. Back then it was either that you sucked at whatever sport was being played or that folks thought you weren't "manly" enough, or as manly as a boy could be. The *audacity* of society to infuse "manhood" into a child's life.

Making do is what I did for years, but rather than let football be my ultimate sport of choice, I found a new love in track and field. It was a sport that didn't require a whole lot of masculinity, and running was something I actually enjoyed doing. I got very involved with track and field in middle school. Although we didn't have an official team, there was a major track meet held with all the middle schools every year. The gym teachers were allowed to choose the best students, and I was chosen both years.

I ended up running varsity for my last three years in high school. I was the main hurdler on the team, and in my senior year, I scored the most points for us. I was proud about that. I even had my time printed in the newspaper once.

It was all a deflection, but a necessary one. I would sometimes use sports as my shield against conversations with my family about the elephant in the room. Instead of "Are you dating?" the question was "How is track going?" A much easier topic for me to handle.

Finding happiness is important. Sometimes it takes pushing yourself past your own boundaries to get to that place. Even though my introduction to sports started from a place of fight or flight, I feel like it opened up some fears I was likely repressing. It wasn't that I had a disdain for sports as much as I had a fear of interacting with people I wasn't comfortable around. It was why I could love video games about sports but hate having to physically participate in them. Running track helped me to see that I could pursue a sport and remain safe *and* be myself.

As an adult Black queer person, I now get teased for how into sports I am. It's always been a running joke that gays don't do sports, which is a lie in most circumstances. I don't have to be confined to an identity that boxes me into a space where I have to choose one or the other. To do so would just reward the homophobia. I can be good at football *and* double Dutch. I am actually still very good at football and double Dutch. But most importantly, I'm not bound by either of them. You don't have to be either.

CHAPTER 5

"HONEST ABE" LIED TO ME

From kindergarten through sixth grade, I attended F. W. Cook, a school that sits on top of a hill in Plainfield, New Jersey. There is this long driveway in front of the school that we would have to walk up. Every winter, every year, the students would plant tulips along the side of it, so we could see them bloom in the spring. Despite the early trauma from the fight in kindergarten, I actually enjoyed my time there. I can remember our school song like it was yesterday:

"Here nestled in the woodside,
Its tower gleaming bright,
There's a schoolhouse quaint and charming
where we learn what is right,
and when our childhood's over,
we'll work with rule or book,
our thoughts will drift to happy days,
we spent at Frederick Cook!"

Cook School was a staple in my family and it was a home for us. The Elders and the Johnsons? We *ran* the school. Or at least we thought we did. Rall, Rasul, me, and my little brother all went during overlapping years. Then we had my cousins Rick and Bernard, who also attended, plus several people who were in Nanny's nursery at one point in time. (Nanny was *always* taking care of other people's children.) We were a unit and we moved as such. We were taught that family protects family—and that's what we did.

I remember how the hallways were lined with posters of historical figures. George Washington, Albert Einstein, Thomas Jefferson, and Benjamin Franklin were a key part of our education as we learned about some of the greatest minds and leaders our country had ever known.

Despite my school consisting of mostly Black students, there were only a few Black faces on the walls of our hallways, like Martin Luther King Jr., Harriet Tubman, and Rosa Parks, each alternating with white historical figures. I remember how I saw all the "good" white and Black figures as being the same. Men like Jefferson and Washington were taught to us in a way that glossed over the fact that they owned slaves—while someone like Robert E. Lee was painted in a much different light for supporting those same things. History has a funny way of painting.

Although we were taught to love and adore Abe Lincoln for freeing us from slavery, I never once questioned why a hundred years later, Martin Luther King Jr. was still fighting for our civil rights.

However much we focused on the older white faces in American history, there was always one time of the year that was dedicated to us Black students. I recall that the few white students we had always seemed a bit out of place on February 1. It was like the tables had turned for a change, and we got to be the center of attention.

My K-12 education mirrored many other systems that oppress the Black community—with Black children being taught by predominantly white staff. From the principal down to the guidance counselor, we were surrounded by white authority figures in my elementary school. We had a minimal number of Black teachers, but Black folks were always the janitors, lunch ladies, and secretaries, which wouldn't be a problem if they also held positions of power. Obviously, there is nothing wrong with any of those jobs, but it would have been even better to see Black people as our teachers and administrators, too. Our being the "center of attention" meant we got to learn about people that looked like us for a change.

On January 31, the hallways were a mix of American history, including a few Black faces we should all know about. By the time we got to school on February 1, it was as if the ancestors had visited overnight and turned the hallways into an homage to Black history. You know that feeling when there's nothing under the tree on Christmas Eve and you wake up Christmas Day with a tree full of presents? *That* was Black History Month for us. Twenty-eight (or sometimes twenty-nine) straight days of Christmas.

Black History Month was Black joy. I took so much pride in learning about my history, as did most of the other students. I remember one time when we had to read about a historical Black figure—I chose Malcolm X. We then had to cut up a brown paper bag and make it into a vest. On the vest, we had to write words and sentences about the person, like important dates and details from their life story. We then stood in front of the class and presented our "Black hero."

It made me feel like I could one day be someone *known* to the world, although I had no idea what I would be known for. Thinking back on it, I always had this feeling inside that I would be somebody. Not just a banker or a lawyer, but someone that everyone knew. It's an important reminder of just how important it is for Black kids to see themselves in the subjects they learn and the people they learn it from. You sometimes don't know you exist until you realize someone like you existed before.

But white teachers were all I knew. Every single teacher I had for my years in elementary school was white. The only Black teachers, Ms. Chiles and Mr. Robinson, had a reputation for having the "bad students." Funny how those classes had only Black students in them. I guess I was being taught to separate myself from my own, just as straight kids were being taught to separate from folk like me. There are levels to the oppression.

Black History Month was always bittersweet, because as quickly as it came it was gone. White history didn't need a month; we were always learning about it. And because we had one teacher teaching various subjects, we learned history every day, but mainly centered around how much the white forefathers did to create the United States. I remember being just as excited about white history, because at the time, it seemed like it was my history, too.

And it was, just not in the way I'd been taught to think.

When I was in the third grade, the school decided to put on a play. It was called something like *This Land Is Your Land* and involved bringing all the students together as historical figures from the past to show unity across different races. Lucky for me, my queerness came off as thespian and I landed the lead role of Abraham Lincoln. Me, a Black kid, getting to play the sixteenth president of the United States, who freed my people. It was a great moment for me, and all my friends were just as excited about it.

At our school, the gym doubled as the auditorium. It had typical basketball court flooring with a stage in the back, which was used for things like award ceremonies and the spelling bee. That day, the gym became my stage. Chairs were placed all over the gym floor to accommodate the large crowd. It was showtime. Although I was nervous, I knew my lines and I was ready to deliver them.

The play started with a depiction of Thanksgiving. Back then, we were taught that everybody got along, including the American Indians and the Pilgrims. I have this image of a poster they used to hang on the wall around Thanksgiving time ingrained in my head. It showed American Indians sharing food with the Pilgrims at the first Thanksgiving.

takes deep breath

What it doesn't show is that the Pilgrims stole the American Indians' food when they first arrived on the *Mayflower*, because they weren't prepared for winter. And many American Indians died from the diseases brought by white settlers. "Peace" was often a survival tactic.

exhales

American history is truly the greatest fable ever written.

Then the play quickly moved to the Revolutionary War and the early founding of the United States. Black kids and white kids were dressed up as Washington, Franklin, Jefferson, and others to give their speeches. There was a reenactment of the signing of the Declaration of Independence and the Constitution.

Finally, to close the show, I was to take center stage and deliver lines from the Emancipation Proclamation, even though the play never touched on slavery. I wore a jacket decorated with red, white, and blue glitter; a felt top hat; and a fake beard. I also wore a pair of suspenders. I was the full embodiment of the USA. Once I finished, we all came together to recite a poem in unison.

I remember how happy I was in that moment. How full of pride I was, thinking that I was playing the man who had done more for my people than any civil rights icon or president in history. Thinking that part of the reason he was murdered was because he decided to free all those who were enslaved, thereby offering me the opportunity—over 140 years later—to sit side by side with white students and teachers.

I used to defend Abraham Lincoln. I remember the teacher showing us the quarter, nickel, dime, and penny. Showing us how on the first three coins, all the presidents look toward the left, while on the penny, Lincoln's face looks toward the right.

Almost as if they were turning their backs on him.

He was placed on the lowest denomination and the only denomination of color, copper. Abraham Lincoln was sold to me as a man who truly cared about Black people, and I don't remember a single Black student back then who didn't hold him in the highest regard.

By fourth grade, we were still learning about American history. We were asked to research Paul Revere at some point. Paul Revere was famous for warning his fellow colonists of the approaching British troops, which would start the Revolutionary War. Our teacher asked us to form groups and come up with a poem to describe the event.

Little did my group members know at the time, but I was secretly a rapper. Story time! I did tell y'all this book would be full of them, right? Uncle Rall, my mom's brother, was an actual rapper, though. He was called the Raw Street Poet Rap Rall Supreme. He looked just like Rakim (look him up if you need to, but just know that he is hip-hop royalty). We used to go with him throughout Jersey as he did shows and events. He even shot a music video once. My older cousins Rall and Rasul could legitimately rap as well. I guess you could say it was in our DNA.

So instead of doing a poem, I made my group do a rap. I wrote all the lyrics to the rap and taught them how to flow. There were two white boys in our group and I remember them struggling, but me and another Black kid got them up to par. We went in front of the class and my friend started beatboxing. I led off—since I wrote it: "Listen up closely and you will hear, the meaning of the story of Paul Revere."

We each had a verse, and then we all came in together on the chorus. The entire class clapped for us when we were done. The rap was so good that the next day, our teacher made us go from classroom to classroom doing the rap for the entire school. Again, it was easy to pay homage back then to white historical figures because we learned about them through the lens that they were concerned about us all.

The interesting thing about studying history is how much it starts to change based on the school setting and who is teaching it. And it's not always about how those teachers view history, but how they view you. And your place in history.

The history I learned in elementary school began to unravel once I hit junior high. Here, all my teachers were Black, and the population of students was overwhelmingly Black. We began learning history that was inclusive of slavery, as well as those historical figures like Washington and Jefferson and how they had some not-so-great history to them. We had teachers who wanted to make sure we really knew what it meant to be Black in America. This was at the Ronald H. Brown School of Global Issues.

In 1992, Ronald Brown was serving as the chairman of the Democratic National Committee, playing an integral role in getting Bill Clinton elected president for his first term. For that, he would be asked to join the president's cabinet as the secretary of commerce, becoming the first African American to ever hold that position. It's important that I say this, because the white community has long prevented Black progress in every arena. Even today, institutions are still having "the first Black person to . . ." And it means something.

It meant something when Halle Berry won the Oscar for Best Actress—still the only Black woman to do so. It was seen as progress when Hattie McDaniel became the first Black woman to ever win for Best Supporting Actress, but needed a special exemption to enter a whites-only building to accept her Oscar because of the venue's adherence to Jim Crow–era segregation laws. It meant something when Obama became the first Black president, 219 years after George Washington, a slave owner, became the first white president—or 145 years after Abraham Lincoln signed the Emancipation Proclamation. Symbolism gives folks hope. But I've come to learn that symbolism is a threat to actual change—it's a chance for those in power to say, "Look how far you have come" rather than admitting, "Look how long we've stopped you from getting here."

Unfortunately, Ron Brown's life would come to a tragic end while he was on a trade mission in April 1996, when a plane carrying him and thirty-two others crashed into a mountainside in Croatia. In his honor, my city created a school dedicated to him. It was the least we could do for a "Black first" who would likely be forgotten one day. Students had to apply and be accepted, even though it was a public school. Attending that school meant a lot for the students, as well as the teachers who taught there. The focus of the school was to build future leaders like Ron.

The administrators wanted to make sure they got it right. There was much less emphasis on white American history in favor of African American history. We learned about slavery, but not just as a CliffsNotes version beside the Civil War. We learned what our people had actually been through and how those things continued to play a role in the current society we lived in.

We learned that Abraham Lincoln wasn't all he was cracked up to be. We learned about the Emancipation Proclamation, but also read some of the statements he made that weren't in the history books. The ones that were disparaging toward Black Americans and the fight for equality. The statements that explained why we needed Martin Luther King Jr., Malcolm X, Medgar Evers, and every other Black activist over a hundred years later, because freeing the slaves didn't really free us.

We learned that Lincoln had many thoughts that never seemed to make it into the pages of the history books. To quote Kandi from *The Real Housewives of Atlanta*, my feelings were "the LIES, the LIES, THE LIES!":

- "My paramount object in this struggle *is* to save the Union, and is *not* either to save or to destroy slavery. If I could save the Union without freeing *any* slave I would do it, and if I could save it by freeing *all* the slaves I would do it; and if I could save it by freeing some and leaving others alone, I would also do that."

- "I will say in addition to this that there is a physical difference between the white and black races which I believe will forever forbid the two races living together on terms of social and political equality."

- "And inasmuch as they cannot so live, while they do remain together there must be the position of superior and inferior, and I as much as any other man am in favor of having the superior position assigned to the white race."

- "I will say then that I am not, nor ever have been, in favor of bringing about in any way the social and political equality of the white and black races."

- "I have no purpose, directly or indirectly, to interfere with the institution of slavery in the States where it exists. I believe I have no lawful right to do so, and I have no inclination to do so."

Junior high was an interesting time for me because I was suppressing my queer identity as hard as possible while also embracing my Black identity. A Black identity that was making me more radical in my thoughts as a teenager and more willing to push back against the whitewashing of Black history.

There was a constant struggle with this type of double living. For me to be Black, and be fully present, I always felt that I had to push myself to be straight. I had on my mask, replete with smiles and laughter to hide my tears. A mask that many Black folk have worn.

"We wear the mask that grins and lies,
It hides our cheeks and shades our eyes,—
This debt we pay to human guile;
With torn and bleeding hearts we smile,
And mouth with myriad subtleties."

Paul Laurence Dunbar wrote words that spoke directly to my soul. He was another one of those heroes that got extra shine during Black History Month. I wonder if the people teaching us this literature knew how many kids were actually experiencing it.

Leaving junior high, I had a whole new outlook on Black history and race in this country. Even though I was only fourteen, I was well aware of what it meant to be a Black "man" in the eyes of society. It wasn't lost on me how racist the Rodney King beating was. Or how divided the world was shown to be with the O. J. Simpson verdict—which many in the Black community saw as a win against a justice system that rarely, if ever, would let a Black man get off. Especially one accused of killing a white woman. Abner Louima's case happened in New York, and it was daily news where I lived. Four cops assaulted him and stuck a plunger in his rectum. Even as a teen, I understood how harsh things could be for me as a person growing from a Black boy to a Black man.

Though my dad was a cop, he knew that being his child wouldn't protect me from how police interacted with Black boys. So my parents taught me early about how you behave so that you don't end up a statistic. "The talk" is what we call it in Black families. Not about the birds and the bees, but about the dangers of interacting with non-Black people, because they will assume the worst of you as a Black boy.

My mom always raised us to be pro-Black, something that other family members used to worry about. The worry wasn't so much that we were going to be the next Angela Davis or Huey Newton, but whether we were old enough to hear such harsh truths. I wish more parents did this, though, at least from the historical standpoint: making sure Black kids come home to read Black literature and know their heritage in depth. 'Cause it damn sure isn't taught to us in school.

I recall Mom saying, "My children are gonna know their history. You just can't be so trusting of white people with your history." I never felt that my mom despised our traditional education; I just think that she knew we needed more. These sentiments were echoed by my father, who worked on a predominantly white police force.

My favorite story of Nanny's was about Big Nanny, her grandmother. One night, the Klan showed up at her doorstep, trying to scare her and her family. Big Nanny pulled out her gun. Nanny always told the story about how Big Nanny knew who it was under the sheets because she could see their shoes. She had cleaned those shoes earlier that day; it was one of the white men she worked for as a maid.

When you have that type of blood running through your veins, you learn that standing in the face of fear is a part of your DNA. I would need all of that and more as I entered high school.

Overnight, I went from being in the majority population of students to being in the minority. I was one of the token Black kids at the Bishop George Ahr High School in Edison, New Jersey, a Catholic school that was primarily white and Filipino. This change in the racial makeup occurred because I went from public to private school. And not only did you need to have certain grades to get in there, but you needed a *certain amount of coins*. Racism was common at my high school, but mainly covert. I was never called a nigger, but I did deal with weird, racially charged questions:

"Are you in the hood?"

"Is your family from the ghetto?"

"Is that your real hair? Can I touch it?"

Microaggression is the academic term for what I was experiencing. Simply put, it's when a person insults or diminishes you based solely on the marginalized group you are in. It's called "micro" because that person isn't outright calling you a n**** or a fa* or both. Instead, they're calling attention to your differences in a low-key way. At times it can seem almost innocent or naïve, but make no mistake, these small things become big over time. These little assumptions grow to create an entire stereotype. This kind of microaggressive behavior often leads to overt racism or homophobia, eventually.

Sometimes it's intentional, like non-Black kids asking questions with a negative, condescending type of vibe to rattle you. But other times, a person doesn't even know that they've insulted you or your culture. You must remember: No matter how it comes at you, the impact matters more than the intent. You are not some lab rat on display. If someone asks you a question and you have to squint your eyes and twist your face a little to make sure you heard them correctly, you've probably just dealt with a microaggression.

My worst experience with this happened when I was in tenth grade. We were in an American history class and going over the usual topics: Washington, Jefferson, and now slavery—because even when my high school did decide to teach Black history outside of Black History Month, it focused on that one subject. Like clockwork, our syllabus went from Slavery to Emancipation, to the Women's Rights Movement, to the Civil Rights Movement, to the final refrain, "Look how far y'all have come." The difference this time around was that I was almost sixteen years old and I had questions. As the teacher started describing slavery, he talked about it as "a thing of its time," and I took issue with that.

You'll find that people often use the excuse "it was the norm" when discussing racism, homophobia, and anything else in our history they are trying to absolve themselves of. Saying that something was "a norm" of the past is a way not to have to deal with its ripple effects in the present. It removes the fact that hate doesn't just stop because a law or the time changed.

Folks use this excuse because they are often unwilling to accept how full of phobias and -isms they are themselves—or at least how they benefit from social structures that privilege them.

This comment was no different, and it was happening in a classroom. *My* classroom! I was still very sassy and opinionated in high school, and my friends and peers looked to me to say what they were afraid to say themselves.

I pressed my teacher hard about why he thought it was okay to simply say that slavery was "a thing of its time." Why didn't he see that people, white people, had made a choice to enslave another race? There were abolitionists who were able to see it was wrong, and Quakers who were able to see it was wrong, so why couldn't all white people see it was wrong?

He responded yet again, saying, "There were many things back then that wouldn't be accepted now. I mean, if I lived during that time, I probably would've had slaves, too."

The class went silent.

I remember how even the white kids looked shocked. It wasn't what he said as much as *how* he said it. So matter of fact. I remember feeling hot. Like, angry hot. When I get really angry, I usually cry, and I could feel myself reaching that level.

Thankfully, I had a friend in the class who spoke up first about her concerns, but it was as though he hadn't heard her.

I finally composed myself enough to respond. "That's not okay. It is not okay for you as a teacher to say that you would have had slaves." He kept trying to go back and forth about it before he ended the conversation by saying, "Let's just move on."

I rarely felt afraid to speak up in Catholic school. And I honestly don't know why, other than feeling that if I didn't, then who would? Maybe it was partly teenage rebellion, but it was more likely the beginnings of the activist that I am today. When people ask me how I got into activism, I often say, "The first person you are ever an activist for is yourself." If I wasn't gonna fight for me, who else was? In turn, I became a voice for us all that day.

This environment wasn't like my public school, where we had school fights and students talked back to teachers, who also weren't afraid to go toe to toe with them. The teachers at my Catholic school wanted civility, and if anything in the classroom made them feel "afraid," they would call for security in a heartbeat. No wonder so many kids of color and queer kids don't feel they have the opportunity to speak for themselves. This double standard is called the "school-to-prison pipeline" nowadays, and it underscores how Black kids are given harsher penalties for the same offenses as white kids. Back then, it was business as usual. Suffice it to say, when white kids spoke up, it was taken as nonthreatening, but when Black kids spoke up, it was clearly different.

Whether it be for personal safety reasons or knowing that it would be taken as a sign of disrespect when a Black child questions a white teacher or person in authority, there are valid reasons why we don't speak up. But it is important to know that if something bothers you that deeply, you have every right to contest it. Only you know how far you are willing to go for yourself.

When I say that Honest Abe lied to me, I mean that the history I once loved as a child wasn't the real history at all. I was educated to believe that Lincoln, and many of the other white historical figures, played little to no role in the oppression Black people have faced for hundreds of years. When we hear the media use the term *alt-history*, it is in direct correlation to what America has always been.

All that I knew about white history as a child had been disproved by the time I became a young adult. The biggest thing I took away from that transformation was to question anything that seemed to have a hole in it. If a story doesn't add up, don't be afraid to ask the tough questions. If those teaching the information are unwilling to give you the answer, you go and do the research yourself.

Anytime I'm dealing with something personally, I look to see which ancestor before me already discussed it. I don't let their work dictate my every action, but I know that I am in a much better postion when I am informed by their work. I use my history as a tool to fight against my marginalization.

The greatest tool you have in fighting the oppression of your Blackness and queerness and anything else within your identity is to be fully educated on it.

Knowledge is truly your sharpest weapon in a world hell-bent on telling you stories that are simply not true.

Honest Abe lied to you.

I won't.

CHAPTER 6

YOU CAN'T SWIM IN COWBOY BOOTS

The last day of school was always the best day of the year as a kid. Besides my birthday, and Christmas, it marked the day where there was no more homework, no more getting up early, no tests, no stress, just fun. Of course, because school is school, they still assigned me several books that I had to read over the summer, which I always waited to work on until the very last week of summer vacation.

Because my parents worked, and as a preteen I wasn't yet old enough to stay home by myself with Garrett, they would put us in those boring-ass Plainfield summer camps. It was not so much the staff that was boring as the activities. There was reading time, and an arts and crafts time, and every Friday we went on a trip to either the zoo or the aquarium. And maybe we weren't even bored with the activities. Maybe it was that we had just gone through nine months of structure in school and didn't want to go right back into more structure.

These summer camps would last about half the summer. The second half of the summer, we all became Nanny's responsibility again. By this time, Rall and Rasul were teenagers, so they weren't around as much. They had gotten jobs, and gotten girlfriends, and gotten too busy to be bothered with me and Garrett all the time.

However, every year Nanny would take all the grandchildren on a summer vacation. One week away from Jersey and the parents. Just her and her grandkids touring the country by plane, train, or automobile. I really miss those trips. I definitely took them for granted.

Looking back, the trip to California will always be my favorite vacation that she took us on. For many of us, it was our first time on a plane. It felt like we were in the air forever, although it had only been six hours.

We got to switch seats, look out the windows at the clouds, and annoy most of the passengers. We were going to California to visit my aunt Audrey, who also happens to be me and Garrett's godmother.

A distinct memory from California was a moment in my aunt's swimming pool. My cousin Cierra, Rall and Rasul's stepsister, came with us on this trip. We were all in the pool one afternoon. Although she had on floaties, something made Cierra panic and start to think she was drowning.

Little Rall swam over to help her. As he tried to calm her down, she continued flailing—so much so that he also began struggling to stay above water. Rasul and I noticed and swam out to the middle of the pool and pushed them both to the side.

Until I started writing this book, I always remembered that moment as a funny one. But now I'm realizing it likely triggered my fear of the water. Following that day, when I would go to kids' pool parties, I would rarely get in or I would just stay in the shallow end, away from all the other kids who could swim.

Our time in California remains one of my best memories because it was where my true bond with Nanny began. While out there, she decided that she was going to buy us all new sneakers before we went to Disneyland the next day. It was around the summer of 1992 or 1993, and Cross Colours was the hottest brand out. All the kids just had to have Cross Colours. Except for me.

As we went through the sneaker store, my cousins all knew they were getting the new Cross Colours, and they did. When Nanny looked at me for my sneaker choice, I told her I didn't want sneakers.

"Well, what *do* you want?" Nanny asked.

"Cowboy boots."

My cousins looked at me like I had an extra eye on my face. But Nanny never flinched. She just waited and assessed the scene. Aunt Audrey said, "Matt, you sure you want cowboy boots?"

I stated my preference again. "Yeah, I want some cowboy boots."

By now my cousins were all trying to save me from myself. They had both grabbed their new Cross Colours out of the box and had them in my face as they said, "But, Matt, these are the hottest sneakers out. We can all look alike!" They were basically pleading with me to get those sneakers. I liked them, don't get me wrong, but I was drawn to having cowboy boots.

At this point, I was becoming visibly frustrated because I felt no one was hearing me. "I don't want sneakers, I want cowboy boots." I was on the verge of tears. As you know, crying is what I do when rage is building up inside of me. Nanny saw it, though, and without hesitation said, "If Matt wants cowboy boots, then we are getting Matt cowboy boots. Audrey, take us to where we can get Matt some cowboy boots." I smiled instantly, and Nanny smiled back at me. Every once in a while, they could get a smile out of me. And off we all went to get me some cowboy boots.

When we got to the store, it was one of those Western-themed places. We were for certain the only Black people in there. My cousins just couldn't believe it, but my face lit up as soon as I entered. I quickly took a look around and there they were: black boots with silver tips—white threading throughout. "I want *these*," I said. They were the best thing I had ever seen. The silver tips were so shiny that you could see your reflection in them. They were odd, but they matched me. They stood out and allowed me to express the parts of me that were different. I fought hard to fit in, but my spirit fought harder to be out. This was my little way of letting it out.

Nanny got the store clerk and asked him to get my boots in a size three. He was a tall white man wearing brown cowboy boots and a cowboy hat. It was as if he had just walked out of a Western film. He had a Southern accent and was very pleasant. Once I tried on my boots, I didn't want to take them off. They came up about calf-high, and they had a little heel on them that made a clacking noise when I walked. They felt so perfect. They spoke to the boy and girl in me. Cowboys were manly, but the heel reminded me of my mother in her heels. They were the best of both worlds.

However, Nanny insisted that I put my sneakers back on, that I could wear my boots the next day. So, I put my boots away in their box, and carried them out of the store with a grin on my face. The next day, I got to be the most embarrassing cousin as we walked through Disneyland all dressed in the same shirts and the same shorts—but they had their new sneakers on and I had my cowboy boots. I was always meant to stand out. Despite how angry they were at how ridiculous I may have looked, I was happy that day.

It was during the summer of 1997 when Nanny decided that she wanted to travel down the East Coast, from Jersey to South Carolina—making stops in Virginia with a final destination of Myrtle Beach, South Carolina.

It was me, Garrett, Rall, Rasul, and my aunt Munch along for the journey this time. When you were on vacation with Nanny, you never knew what was in store. We always got to go shopping, do all the amusement parks, wake up early, stay up late, and generally enjoy ourselves.

I remember her telling us that we were blessed, because many kids didn't get to have these types of experiences. Many kids never leave their state, or get to leave their city for that matter. Nanny never wanted that for her children, and she certainly didn't want it for us. She made sure we not only got to be kids but that we were afforded luxuries that many of our white classmates had.

When we finally made it to Myrtle Beach, we all went to the Pavilion to play games and walk the boardwalk. Miniature golf was on the schedule the next day. Nanny got ready after lunch, and so did all of us boys. The last person we were waiting for was Aunt Munch. So, we waited. Half an hour. An hour. One and a half hours. It seemed like it was two hours later when she finally came out. We all laughed because she didn't look much different than before, but that was Aunt Munch: cool, smart, quirky, and always taking her time. Nanny hated it.

We went miniature golfing that night and had a great time. Well, we had a great time *after* we got past the first hole. I was up first, and it was also my first time with a golf club. Now, I had assumed that what I saw on TV was how I should swing a club in real life. Unfortunately, those around me weren't prepared for my golfing skills, including Aunt Munch's face. I took a big swing like Tiger Woods, and knocked her glasses clear off her face.

She was mad at first, but quickly got over it and simply said, "You don't have to do all that." I apologized and swung much more gently on the second go-round. When we got back to the hotel, it wasn't too late, and Nanny said we could go to the hotel pool for a little while since it was well lit.

Me, Rall, and Rasul walked down to the pool and stood at the deep end, which was ten feet. It was either Rall or Rasul who said, "Matt, you still wanna learn how to swim?" They were actually both really good swimmers, and like the big cousins they were, they wanted to make sure I knew how to swim as well. I swear our growing up was like a scene from the movie *Stand by Me*, but with four little Black boys as the leads. Or maybe *Family Guy* is a better reference? Either way, it was always an adventure.

I looked at them and stupidly was like, "Yeah."

"Well, swim!"

And then there was a push. And then there was a large splash. And then there was me coming up for air.

If your heart just stopped, it's because this sounds as dangerous as it actually was. For starters, I really did not know how to swim. It had been only a few years since the California trip. In pools, I either stayed in the shallow end or I wore arm floats if I ever went near the deep end. This was a very real situation, and I was scared.

I was out there in ten feet of water by myself as the two of them stood over me and watched. At first, I panicked—but it was only for a short time before I realized I was staying afloat. My fight to not drown was outweighing my fear of not knowing how to swim. I just kept kicking below and flailing up top. I wasn't moving anywhere, but I wasn't drowning either.

After about forty-five seconds, they both jumped in and treaded water next to me. They were smiling that proud big-cousin smile. Eventually, they pushed me over to the edge of the pool, so I could catch my breath. One moved to the deep end, and the other stayed in the shallow end. That night, they had me swim back and forth across the deep end between them. They weren't worried about enjoying themselves. It was more important to them that I knew how to swim.

Back and forth I went—each time across getting better and better, my fear subsiding with each paddle, my confidence growing with each completed lap. As ridiculous as their teenage logic was (and I would never recommend it), it worked. They pushed me in the water that night and stayed with me until I conquered one of my greatest fears.

It was very late when we finally got out of the pool and went back upstairs to our room. I was so excited about my accomplishment, and they were, too. In their rough and tough roundabout way, they taught me how to swim. But really, they were teaching me how to fight for myself—with the reminder that they would always be there to support me when I needed them.

And they were *always* there for me throughout most of my childhood and early teenage years. When we got jumped, they were still there fighting to the very end to protect me. Even when I got the cowboy boots, they didn't like it, but they would also dare anyone else to threaten their weird cousin.

I could've easily drowned that night. In Rose Hackman's article in the *Guardian* on post-segregation public swimming pools, she explains how Black kids drown at roughly three times the rate of white kids due to a lack of resources, both tangible and cultural, as well as racism. It's interesting how many things in this country white kids do as a given but Black kids continue to struggle with for generations. Black folks have always had a complicated connection to water, and even a fear of it dating back to our enslavement.

My ancestors were brought here on boats, stowed away in holds without being able to see anything. But they could hear water beating on the hull outside. I imagine that the last sound many of my ancestors heard was the rush of water. Even when the enslaved were able to break free from their shackles, many of them chose to jump overboard and die at sea rather than be held in bondage.

Consider recent American history: After the integration of public swimming pools, pools were filled with cement or simply closed in predominantly Black areas. This prevented Black families and their children from learning to swim. That is the type of social pathology that runs through us. Find a flaw, deficit, or disadvantage in our community, and I can find a system that oppressed us and made it that way.

It's why I think that everything in our past is important and plays a role in our future. Watching my cousin almost drown prevented me from swimming. When I got older, I learned that my mother almost drowned and that she rarely goes near swimming pools. Which is likely why she didn't invest in us learning to swim—she simply didn't see it as a necessity. Everything is connected, and it often requires someone breaking a stigma or pattern in order to change the trajectory of a family.

Instead of giving up and drowning, I fought to stay afloat. Much like I had done with my life at that point:

Anytime I was pushed down, I got back up. Vacations with Nanny and her boys were usually a reprieve from the daily struggle of being myself. It removed me from the environment that I didn't fit into and brought me to a place where there was nothing but love. Love for the person I was, without limitations.

Every day when I wake up, it's like being pushed in that pool again. For more than thirty years, I've decided to swim instead of drowning. I know so many Black and queer folks that stopped swimming when the waves got too rough and the water got too heavy. So many who weren't given the proper teaching or protection to survive.

The real question we must each ask ourselves every day is: *Am I willing to swim?* Or is this the day that you drown? Many times, this decision will be in our own hands. Sadly though, in a world that continues to kill Black queer people every day, that decision isn't always ours to make. But I swim anyway. Every single morning, I put on my goggles and dive right into the deep end of racism, homophobia, and every other oppression that is thrown my way.

There just don't seem to be enough Little Ralls,

Rasuls, and Nannys in the world willing to reach their hand into the water to pull us to safety. Too many watch in silence while others in the community suppress Black queer people. One day the choice must be made by all: Are you teaching people how to swim or are you letting them drown?

Officer Gregory Johnson (father) sworn in as a sergeant, Plainfield Police Department, with sons G.G. (older brother) and George

ACT 2

FAMILY

DEAR LITTLE BROTHER,

Thank you. I know as Black boys and men, we are not conditioned to share emotions in this way. So, for those who read this, I hope it will be an important display of love.

Love isn't a word that we have to use with each other, because for us it has always been an action. We have always been able to show our love for each other through our care. Through our ability to often be on the same page. And even if we aren't, through our ability to get right back on it within hours.

My memories of you are likely as old as my memories of myself. You were there for my entire adolescence, until I went away to college. As boys, our parents kept us close. Even though we were three years apart, we never let that separate us. We played sports with the neighborhood kids together, rode bikes together, and actually hung out together. Not because we had to, but because we wanted to.

Now, time to embarrass you some. I remember you had a nickname, "Moot." I used to think that was so cool, but you hated being called that by the time you were seven. You also hated your middle name, Samuel.

Another name I liked—ha! I always admired that about you, though. You were never afraid to say what you were thinking or how something made you feel. From a very young age, you were able to make your own decisions in a way that I struggled to.

I remember us as little kids taking baths together. Playing in the bubbles with action figures until our skin got extra wrinkly. Then getting out and getting ready for bed. We always had bunk beds, and of course I got the top because I was older. But I always felt bad about it, because even though I wanted the top bunk, I also wanted you to be happy. I guess that's why I let you control the TV. Watching *SportsCenter* ALL DAY AND NIGHT was part of what got me to start liking and understanding sports. I'd always wait until you fell asleep to turn on Nick at Nite so I could watch my old shows like *Dick Van Dyke* and *I Love Lucy*. I was so damn weird.

Although I know I don't have to, because you would never require it, I want to apologize for all the heat you took just for being my brother. Because I know what I dealt with all my life in being called a faggot and other mistreatments, and I can only imagine how that was projected onto you. Not in the sense that anyone would call you that, but that folk would likely use me as a way to get under your skin. As much as I tried to hide my identity, I know it was easily seen by most.

Part of that guilt forced me to overcompensate in certain areas of our relationship. I knew I lacked what you needed from me in other areas. I couldn't talk with you about girls or show you the ropes, because I had no experience. The same way Daddy expressed his affection through gifts, I in turn did the same with you. But know that I always wanted to. I always enjoyed making sure that you had what you needed, from your first car to when you Jedi-mind-tricked me with your famous "Don't you wanna buy these for me?" text messages (which I know you know still work on me).

I wanted to write this letter so that others who may be in a similar situation can read it. A brother or sister who is growing up with a member of the LGBTQIAP+ community in their own household. It could have been very easy for you to shy away from me or disown me as a way to protect yourself. But instead, you leaned in—and hard. You defended me when you felt it was necessary and never once called me out of my name, even if others around you were doing so.

You are living proof that it really isn't as hard as most think to get along with and enjoy the company of people from different sexual identities. From brothers who took baths together, to brothers playing ball together, *whispers* smoking weed together, and now spending time talking while you sip on Hennessy and I, white wine. We are still very different and very much the same all at once.

Most importantly though, I wanted to write this because we both now have an even greater purpose on this earth. Although we will be the shining example of what hetero/homo brotherhoods look like, we have been blessed with something even more important: The birth of your first child, who we affectionately call Baby G, your junior. Since Baby G has come into our lives, I can already see the change in you as well as the changes in myself.

I sometimes sit as I'm holding him and think to myself, *Who is Baby G gonna end up like?* Will he be like his mother's side of the family? Will he be like you? My greatest worry is that he will be like me. Not because there is anything wrong with that, but because I know how the world can treat boys like me. I also know that it is my duty to protect him regardless of how Baby G turns out to be, because Black babies are born into oppression despite any additional marginalizations.

I also know that it doesn't matter how Baby G's personality turns out, because he has you—someone who is already well equipped to know what can come when boys don't fit a specific mold, like your brothers. You have always operated from a place of love. You saw that I was gay, but that it was only one piece of me. You have always done an amazing job of seeing me as fully human—something I wish others in our community learned to do better. My queer identity is a part of my Blackness, and you never made me separate the two.

I'm excited about the next steps in our journey together. I take joy in knowing that I did my very best as your older brother, and that we now get to impart our experiences to the newest addition to our family. You're going to be an amazing father. Just remember that you will always be my first baby.

CHAPTER 7

NANNY:
THE CAREGIVER, THE HUSTLER, MY BEST FRIEND

"*AT-AT-AT!!!* Elbows off the table when you eat in my house."

"What's taking you so long to play a damn card? Scared money don't make money."

"What did I tell you about staying outta grown folk's business?"

"Listen, Matt. You won't know if you don't like Brussels sprouts until you actually try Brussels sprouts. If you eat them now and you don't like them, you will never have to eat them again. But you will try it at least once."

Louise Kennedy Evans Elder was her full name. I always thought it was funny that my grandmother had three last names. To the world, she was all of those people, but to me and her other grandkids, she was simply "Nanny."

She stood about five foot five, a little heavyset, as I've said, with brown skin. According to the stories, my grandmother's hair went gray when she was sixteen years old, which I always thought was cool. She was the baby of thirteen kids, yet stood as the matriarch to our entire family, even though her siblings were still alive *and* older than her. When she wanted something done, it got done. And if she couldn't get it done, she would assign one of her kids or grandkids to do it. She was always great at delegation.

She was, and still is, the best cook I've ever known. She had the ability to make anything from scratch, as long as she knew the ingredients. One of my favorite memories with her was being one of her helpers in the kitchen during a Thanksgiving dinner and noticing how she didn't use a measuring cup to make anything. She was preparing her famous sweet potato pies with me when I asked her, "Why don't you ever use a measuring cup? Like, how do you know if you put too much or too little in the mix?" She laughed hard, then looked at me and said, "If you use a measuring cup, your food will taste measured. Taste your food while you are cooking it. That's where most people make their mistakes. Get all the way done cooking and then the shit be nasty." We both laughed out loud.

She did cool things like make breakfast for dinner, root beer floats, and homemade ice cream sandwiches. However, she had to make mine a little bit differently than the other grandchildren's. She always microwaved my ice cream for a few seconds just to make sure it was soft. I was the kid who hated for his food to be too cold or too hot. Being a little different was my norm, but she never once wavered in making sure I was properly accommodated, just like the rest of her grandkids. My Lord, I was weird. I have to laugh while writing this.

Whenever us cousins had discussions about who her favorite grandchild was—because there was one cousin who always got very sensitive about this—the conversation was mostly in jest with her in the room.

I think it bothered her that we even felt she wasn't equal with all of us. After a while though, she knew we were just messing around, but her response to all the battling over who her favorite was always ended the same:

"I love all of my grandkids, but I love each of you differently. Because you each need different things."

That "different things" part spoke to my soul.

It wasn't until I was a little older that I realized what this meant, and how well she spread her love to all of us, even when there were times she probably wasn't taking care of herself. To be honest, her whole life has been dedicated to spreading herself so thin that there was rarely much left for herself when she went to bed every night. If we knew then what we know now, we wouldn't have let her pour so much energy into us without pouring some back into her in return. More on that later, though.

Some of my cousins needed a place to call home, as things were a little rough for their parents. Some of us needed a stable environment to come home to every day after school, as our parents worked long shifts. Some of the grandkids needed tough love and strong rules. She provided for all of us.

And then there was me.

A little queer Black boy still very unsure of who he was. I buried myself in schoolwork and hid behind my books. What I didn't have in friendships, I could always find in stories. While other kids were out playing in their respective cliques, I spent my time in the library or doing homework or playing *Jeopardy!* on Nintendo. I entered the Gifted & Talented program in the third grade, which separated out the "smarter" kids from those with average grades.

Using education as a tool of division has a distinct history in Black society. W.E.B. Du Bois highly publicized "the talented tenth" principle, a belief that the top 10 percent of Black intellectuals would lead the other 90 percent out of oppression. Although division of people through intelligence isn't exclusive to the Black community, it has much different connotations when you know that white folks, regardless of where they fall in school, can achieve. Donald Trump went from a reality TV star to being president of the United States. There will always be a different set of standards for us.

When you are the smart one in the Black family, your relatives come to you for everything. It's almost a running joke in our community that you could go to college for one thing, but people will come to you for everything else simply because you are "the educated one." Even to Nanny, education was the key. Her parents weren't educated, so they didn't push it on her, and she in turn wasn't "book educated." So, she made sure we took it seriously.

Knowing I was smart, my grandmother decided to make me her protégé. See, Nanny wasn't just a caregiver and a cook. She was a hustler. Mainstream media tends to make the idea of "the hustle" a bad thing. What many of us in the Black community know as "hustling," gets taught in college business programs as "multiple streams of income."

My grandmother ran a nursery out of her house, which most of the neighborhood kids grew up in. She also baked pies and did catering events across the state. She was a registered nurse and had a wealthy white client that lived in South Jersey, who she would visit twice a week. She also did the flea markets and garage sales. Nanny knew how to keep a check, money in the bank, and cash in the mattress for a rainy day.

I became her sidekick and her business partner, diving into a number of little ventures. One time, we decided I would start a candy business to make extra money for toys, clothes, you name it. We went to the BJ's and bought the candy in bulk. To start, she gave me a one-hundred-dollar loan. With that, I was able to buy up what she called my "stock." When we got home, she made me calculate how many pieces I had, what I needed to sell each piece for, and how much profit I could make. We made a deal that I would pay the loan back weekly, at twenty dollars a week, until it was paid off.

I was selling candy to every kid on the playground, before school and after school. I made a cool hundred slinging Pop Rocks on the yard. The operation lasted for several months before the school caught wind of it. It wasn't illegal to be selling the candy, but the parents complained that their kids kept "coming up short" on their lunch money every week.

For years, my grandmother and I were a team. Slinging Pop Rocks was just one of our many hustles. Every weekend, we would travel to the flea market early in the morning and sell old things from around the house, like porcelain dolls, or pies and cakes she had prepared the night before. It became our weekly thing. I enjoyed hanging with her and haggling with potential buyers, meeting new people, and being out of the house. The days would be long, but fun. She always made sure I had something to do. And there was never a crisis she couldn't fix.

As a kid, I didn't fully take in what it meant to spend time with her. I think about how important every minute I get to spend with her is now and how back then, those minutes felt infinite. I never thought about the day when she would no longer be here in the physical form. She was my grandmother, of course, but more importantly, she was always my friend. She gave me things to be proud of: My ability to help people with less than I had. My ability to make money.

Even when I was in high school, she was always by my side. As freshmen in Catholic school, we were all required to do 250 hours of community service a year. Coming from public school where I never had such requirements, I didn't have a clue about how I was going to achieve that. All the white kids seemed to have internships or volunteer places already lined up to sign their hours away. And my parents—who were already shelling out $5,000 a year for the school—didn't have the capacity to take this on, too. But she did.

Rather than having me find some random organization to work for, she started the Sarah Marsh Missionary Society Soup Kitchen at Mt. Zion AME Church, where we had been members my whole life. She literally started an entire soup kitchen just so I could fulfill my community service hours. Every Saturday morning, we would go to the church, sometimes with other church women, but mostly just us. We would make soup and meals for the sick and shut-in. Then during lunchtime, we would go throughout the city, visiting church members and feeding them. We'd talk with each of them for a few minutes and then go to the next stop. We did this for four years, until she was sure I had enough hours to graduate from high school.

It took me until the end of high school to realize what she was doing with all of this hustling. It wasn't simply that she thought I was smart and should learn how to create income. It wasn't simply because she wanted me to be a caring person that gave back to the community. She wanted me to be all those things, yes, but most importantly, she didn't want me to be alone.

I was becoming isolated around the age of ten, and

she saw it. As hard as I tried to suppress my queer identity and fit in, I just didn't. I had friends, but not how my cousins and brothers had friends. My older cousins had friend circles, and sometimes I could tag along. But I would frequently be too young to hang with them. They would go to parties together, to the local pool, and more often than not, get into fights with other crews *together*. They were a tight unit, but not my unit.

My younger brother had an entire crew as well. When they were little, they would all get the same sneakers. They all joined the same sports leagues so they could hang together. They attended the same elementary, middle, and high school together. Even as adults, they all still live in Plainfield, are each other's children's godparents, and see each other weekly. My brother was the leader then and now.

I had my books.

I had my homework.

I had myself and I was isolated.

Like the natural born caregiver she was, my grand-mother frequently placed me before herself. Even if that meant she was carrying a young child everywhere with her, she wasn't going to let me be alone. Nanny decided that *she* would be my circle. At moments when I needed a best friend, she would be my best friend. I remember the hundreds of times she would play Rummy 500 with me for hours until I was ready to go to bed. The seven a.m. "let's roll" throughout the state to go to the flea markets. We were in it together. Furthermore, she had been in it before with children like me in our family.

Growing up, I had a transgender cousin named Hope, as well as other lesbians and gays within the family. My grandmother watched Hope grow up and transition, and I think that helped her to understand what she was seeing in me. She had also seen the damage that happens when children who are "different" aren't nurtured and loved the same way other kids are. When she says, "I love each of you differently," she doesn't mean *I love you less*, she means *I love you whole, and as you are.*

I often think about what it would be like if the world existed with a "Nanny" in each family. Why was my Black queer experience one of unconditional love when several others have become the standard of hate and familial violence? Although the national rate of homelessness for LGBTQIAP+ youth is near

40 percent, the rate in my family has always been 0 percent. How could one family get so right what the world has gotten so wrong? We should have been the rule. Not the exception.

Instead, the rule looks more like "I'd rather have a dead child than a gay child." That mentality was purportedly held by the father of young Giovanni Melton after killing his son on November 2, 2017. I had a father who never once said anything about how effeminate I was. My mother, who always knew, put a system of family support in place for me from the age of two. She understood I would need people later in life who could relate to my experience—aunts and uncles who loved me, loved me, and loved me even more. Cousins who were always willing to fight for me and siblings who have always had my back.

Family dynamics is a topic that comes up often in LGBTQIAP+ culture. "Created family" is a system in which friends from many walks of life create extremely tight friendship circles in an effort to ensure a familial type of environment for the many who are not accepted at home.

Our culture has always found a way to create safety and refuge where there was none. The television show

Pose depicts pretty accurately how our culture has survived. "Houses" within the ballroom culture were formed as places for LGBTQIAP+ people to go when they had no home. They had a family structure, complete with a house mother whose job it was to look out for her kids.

I wish me and my family had known the various statistics that many LGBTQIAP+ youth fall into. The love I had at home couldn't be found in the other environments I had to navigate daily. As scared as I was to be "out," they were just as scared to ask me if I was gay. So even though they knew about my sexuality, they didn't seek out any additional information about the LGBTQIAP+ culture. In other words, they knew queer when they saw it, but not enough to teach me the ropes and potential pitfalls of it.

Even though I didn't know my queer culture or have the resources to explore it, at least I had a home. I had a home because Nanny ensured it. "Charity starts at home" was one of her favorite sayings. And I know that there are hundreds of other "Nanny"s around the world who fight for little Black boys and girls and gender nonconforming people who are considered different. They notice the signs and step in to make sure that those children know they are loved unconditionally. Nanny didn't just keep her wisdom to herself. She put that in her children, who in turn put that seed in us. They put that seed in me to now be a voice for other Black queer boys who didn't know there was someone out there fighting for them every day.

There are so many people who are young and out and looking for a support system. Build the support system that you want to have around you. This won't always be easy, I'm not going to lie. I won't sell you the fable of "It Gets Better" like media tries to do without offering how. The how comes in being willing to take a chance on yourself and create the support system you wish to have. I would also tell you to reclaim that campaign slogan and use it from a place of power. Tell folks, especially those who are non-queer and non-Black, to "Make it Better." Something getting better doesn't happen without action, and you have every right to ask for that.

The way I grew up always knowing that I would have a friend in Nanny, is the same way I hope Black queer boys, who may never meet me but will hear and see my words, know they always have a friend in me. Sometimes all it takes is someone seeing you as you are. Nanny saw me, I see you, and now you see yourself.

I recall a conversation Nanny and I had later in life, moments after I officially came out to her, when I was about twenty-five. I had always wanted to do it, but I didn't have the full confidence for it until I was older. My fear was that my being gay would disappoint them. Although they gave me no reason to think that, the community I lived in was a different world. One of stigma around HIV, and shaming around gay sexuality. So I waited until *I* felt it was the right time.

There I was, crying on the phone, and she was still just as steady as a rock. Firstly, by affirming me in the moment and telling me I didn't need to cry nor was my being gay an embarrassment to my family. Secondly, by telling me that she always knew and reminding me that "I love all my grandkids, and you know that I love you regardless." The final thing she said, though, is what will always stick with me. "And when you finally start dating a guy, you still gotta do just like all the other grandkids and bring him to meet me before anybody else."

Although that day has still not happened, it was a

reminder that as different as we are as queer people, some things are simply universal regardless of sex, gender, or (insert difference here). Elevating a community viewed as below you to having the same equity and equality harms no one but the oppressor.

Nanny won't win any awards from GLAAD. She won't have her picture hung up during Black History Month, or make any headlines for operating out of a place of love. But because she saw me, I get the chance to tell everyone about her. And maybe, just maybe an LGBTQIAP+ person's family members or peers will read these words and enough of her spirit will rub off.

CHAPTER 8

DADDY'S SECOND CHANCE

"Mattmole frijole, Mattmole frijole, Mattmole frijole!" Daddy would say when he saw me walking through the house. It was his nickname for me. At that time, they called my little brother "Moot"—a nickname that he gave an RIP to at age seven. If you know Garrett, then you know that if he didn't like it, he wasn't going to allow you to say it.

I, on the other hand, enjoyed when my dad called me "Mattmole frijole." He would say it in a roaring voice that would always make me laugh. As a child, my relationship with my dad was very simple. He was a manly man, so to speak, and I was an effeminate child, so we didn't really have too much in common. He wasn't the type to hug you or give you a kiss or tuck you into bed at night. But you always knew that he loved you, and he showed it in different ways.

Christmas, birthdays, and vacations were the clearest ways in which he showed his affection. No expense was ever spared when it came to his kids. When I was growing up, me and my little brother lived in our parents' house. Both our older sister, Tonya, and older brother, Gregory Jr., who we call G.G., primarily lived on their own. Because they were so much older, they only stayed with us during brief stints when they were in between places of their own. That was one thing about my dad. No matter how much you did wrong or pissed him off, you could always come back home. He is still like that to this day.

To understand my dad, and my relationship with him, you need to know his roots. My dad was born and raised in his early years in Williamsburg, Virginia. "A country nigga from the South," as he would call it. My grandmother said he was the first baby born at Williamsburg Hospital. As kids, we used to travel down to the house he grew up in all the time. It had been in the family since 1927, built on a small piece of land that was given to my great-grandfather by the family he worked for. We used to hate taking those trips, but they meant we didn't have to be in Jersey for a few days, so we sucked it up and dealt with it. It was in the country, and there was honestly nothing to do there all day but sit and watch TV. My other grandmother, who we called "Grandma," lived there. She was my dad's mother.

My grandma's home was a shotgun house, and to the back right of it was another small shotgun house that my uncle Tick and aunt Lestine used to live in. Behind that, there were woods. I can remember Grandma always yelling at us that "Y'all better get from out those woods! Get a tick up in them hinepots!!!" It wasn't until I was much older that I realized what she was saying was hind parts, or country slang for "your ass." "Hinepots" just has a much better ring to it, though.

To the back left of Grandma's sat a much larger house. Grandma told us that her father used to work that land back in the 1920s. That the owner of the larger house was the one who gave her father the piece of land to the front, which her shotgun house sat on. Her father built the house with his own two hands—a bathroom in the front, followed by a kitchen with a bedroom to the side, followed by the living room, and the dining room in the back with a second bedroom to the side. If I ever wanted to go visit it now, I would have to park my car where it used to be. All that history is gone now as gentrification has turned that land into a parking lot. I think it was because my dad's family came from such humble beginnings that he never wanted his children to have that same experience.

The house was built in 1927, and Grandma was born in 1928. She and her two brothers were raised in that house. She then had three kids of her own and raised them in that house as well. That little house held so many memories—including several family members who passed away there. As kids, we would be afraid to sleep in the back room. It was always cold, and you could see stuff moving.

Yes. The house had ghosts, and Grandma liked to bring it up from time to time that she could see them. Television has a way of making you think that everyone's last breath is taken in a hospital bed, when many actually pass away in their own homes. Unless the conditions mandated that we had to be in the hospital, folks in our family would request to be at home in their final days so they could be surrounded by family and loved ones.

We would get so scared to sleep in either of the bedrooms in her house because of the ghost stories. Then one day, Grandma asked, "Why y'all afraid of the ghosts?"

We just looked at her like, *Because they are ghosts.*

"Those are your relatives," she explained. "Why would your relatives hurt you? White people taught y'all to be afraid of ghosts. That's why they used to dress up in sheets like them. Ain't no need to be afraid of ghosts of your own people." From the moment she told me that, I never feared sleeping in that house again.

Grandma was a stern woman. A God-fearing churchgoing woman who thought white people were the devil—and she used to say it proudly. She grew up during a time when the world looked a lot different. She was born in the South during the height of Jim Crow laws, which were a set of rules put in place by white lawmakers to govern how "negroes" were to be treated. They were meant to enforce racial segregation. Laws like:

"No person or corporation shall require any white female nurse to nurse in wards or rooms in hospitals, either public or private, in which negro men are placed."

"No colored barber shall serve as a barber [to] white women or girls."

I'm sure she saw some things that I could never even imagine. My father came from her, and because of that, he took on many of her traits. Strong, but caring. You always knew he loved you even if he didn't always know how to show it. Much like my relationship with my grandma.

"Excuse the pig but not the hog, and catch the boy who got the frog." That's my favorite saying of his. Dad would say it every time he burped. He learned a lot of good traits from his upbringing, but with them also came some bad ones. He was pretty patriarchal in his thinking, and being with my mother, who is a very independent woman, must've been a challenge for them both. They didn't fight or argue much in front of us, but he was definitely the king of his castle.

He would do things like leave his plate on the table

instead of clearing it and expect dinner to be cooked every night. That was part of the social conditioning from his upbringing. Grandma used to do that for him and her husband, Tuck. My mother ain't never liked that responsibility. And even though she would do it, she would let him know "you can clean your plate off the table, negro." He would just make a face and move on.

I remember one time when I was a teen, we went to Virginia, and he and his older brother watched my then seventy-plus-year-old grandmother fry them chicken, make their plates, watch them eat, and then clean up after them. I stopped her and said to my father and uncle, "I know y'all not about to have Grandma clean up after y'all."

They both looked up stunned. Not mad at me, but so unused to ever having to clean up after themselves, they almost didn't even notice they were adults. They were children being chastised in that moment. I cleaned the table off that day and let Grandma rest. I just looked at them with a face that said, "You n*****
ought to be ashamed." My dad just sucked his teeth and said, "What?" with his arms open. This was his normal response whenever he felt he was right.

Grandma would follow the tradition like her aunts and uncles before her. She too would pass away in that house, being the last to ever do so. I think there's something to be said for dying on your own terms in your own house and having your ancestors be there to take you home. She was surrounded by her children when she took her last breath, right there in the living room on the daybed I used to sleep in when I would visit as a teenager. Her passing away was only the second time I've seen my father cry—the first time being when my uncle Rhem passed in 2004.

My older brother, G.G., and sister, Tonya, have a different mom from Garrett and me. My dad was married to their mother, Sheila, for ten years before they divorced. He has now been married to my mom for over thirty-five years. He has been married for more than half his life. G.G. moved to live with Grandma when he was sixteen. Garrett and I were much closer to Nanny, and G.G. and Tonya were much closer to Grandma. Family dynamics.

G.G. is six foot three, slender, and darker-skinned. He has the most perfect teeth. We didn't really grow up together, but by the time I was a teenager he, Garrett, and I had built a really great brotherhood bond.

We would go to the movies weekly and eat at Applebee's. We had lost a lot of time with him not being around earlier, so we made up for it in those years.

My father and G.G. had an interesting relationship. It wasn't always bad, but it most certainly wasn't always good. They butted heads a lot. From the stories I heard, when my father married my mother, G.G. didn't take it too well. Typical stepmom drama. He and my father began clashing when he was in his teens, and so G.G. went to live with my grandmother in Virginia. He would come back and visit from time to time, but our relationship didn't really become a thing until he was an adult and I was a teen. We are eleven years apart.

It's unfortunate that we lost out on so much time. Had we been brave enough to talk to each other about what we were both feeling, we might've learned how we were much more alike than we knew. My brother G.G. is gay. I think it played a role in the relationship he had with my dad. Having a gay son born in the 1970s who was exhibiting similarly effeminate qualities to what I was exhibiting was likely something my dad struggled to deal with. There was even less queer visibility and representation in the '70s than what

I had in the '90s. G.G. also had a different mother, which played a factor. Whereas my mother's side of the family was known to have queer people, G.G.'s mother might have struggled to know what to do.

I think my father went into raising me much differently a decade later. He had a second chance to get it right this time, to have the relationship he wanted with his eldest son. And I feel that he overcompensated with me in ways that he wasn't able to do for G.G.

As manly as my dad was, he honestly just let me be. Every now and then, if I gravitated toward something that was too girly, he might let the word "sissy" fly. But he never hurled the term at me so much as he hurled it at the thing I was doing.

My favorite memory of him is from a random day at Nanny's. I was about eleven or twelve and was outside playing with the football by myself, throwing the ball up in the air as high as I could and then catching it. He just happened to walk outside to take a call on his cell phone.

After he finished, my dad walked over to me and asked, "You know how to play football?"

I looked at him with the *duh* face and said, "Yeah, I play it every day at school."

"All right, go out for a catch," he responded. I gave him the ball and began running. He waited about five seconds before throwing it to me. There was such a look on his face when he saw me catch it—first shock, then approval. He was even more surprised when I threw the football back with a perfect spiral. This was around the same time I was proving my natural sports ability to kids on the playground. It's interesting how both children and adults assumed I'd have an inability to play "boy" sports simply because I was more effeminate.

My dad was astonished, and I knew it. I think he assumed that because I was the bookworm who really didn't show a lot of interest in sports the way Garrett did, that I didn't participate in them at all. I think a lot of times he saw G.G. in me, and rather than fight against what he was seeing, he decided to not engage with me at all.

That day changed our relationship forever. We stayed out there and played catch as the sun went down. Back and forth we went, as I ran out for passes from him, catching, and returning. Over and over again. There was a lesson in that day for us both: We didn't have to just exist as two people living in the same house together. He wasn't going to like and understand everything that was going on with me, but he didn't have to treat me different because of it. I learned that I could have my father and a relationship with him, too.

He started taking my interest in sports much more seriously. He paid all the fees for me to run track and field. I even joined the bowling team in high school, and as corny as that was for a Black kid, he paid for everything I needed. The shoes, the balls, the fees, all of it. I could feel how much he missed out on with G.G.

I was the only one of his children to go to private school, which he paid for. When I went away to college, he paid my rent and part of my tuition each semester. There was nothing that he wouldn't do for me.

This doesn't mean that everything between us was always perfect, though. We bumped heads plenty of times as I got older and became more independent. There were times he thought he could make decisions for me from 300-plus miles away, which I didn't go for. I would call my mother to vent. Sometimes those calls to her were filled with tears. My mother always assured me that my father cared about me. And she explained that it was hard for him to deal with the fact that I was my own person and that he couldn't make decisions for me as an adult.

I was about to turn twenty-one when I got the call that he had been hospitalized with congestive heart failure. His strength mirrored his stubbornness, especially when it came to his own health. He had a fear of hospitals and doctors, as many Black families do. Medical mistreatment and discrimination have made us distrustful of places responsible for our health. So, we wait till we are damn near dead before we go.

He was literally lying in his bed barely able to breathe when my brother Garrett walked by his bedroom and saw him struggling. Garrett told him, "Either I'm taking you to the hospital or I'm calling the ambulance. But either way, you are going."

We were planning to celebrate my twenty-first birthday in Jersey, and I had brought all my line brothers with me. I was in my final semester of college at Virginia Union University, and the party was supposed to be in Plainfield.

It was about two hours before the party when I went up to the hospital to see him by himself. I just wanted to make sure that he got to see me on my birthday, and I him. I walked into the room and saw him sitting there watching TV with a full-faced oxygen mask on. It was the first time I'd ever seen my father with a scared look on his face. I'm not sure if he was scared by how bad he'd let his health get or scared for me to see him in such a vulnerable state—the strongest man I knew now reduced to that hospital bed.

I sat down beside him for a few minutes—extremely nervous and scared to see him so sick. In that moment, all the little arguments and head-butting we'd been having seemed so frivolous.

"I wish you could come tonight," I said.

"Yeah, me too," he said. He looked so disappointed. I think he realized that the sometimes-selfish man he could be came with a cost, too. Missing this milestone for me was that cost. I assured him that it was okay, and the most important thing was for him to get out of there.

I went on that night to have my twenty-first birthday party with the rest of my family by my side. All of my cousins, the village, and some of their friends came to celebrate me officially becoming an "adult." It was a bittersweet evening. I kept wanting my dad to be there with me. It was a reminder of how we can take people for granted. It's easy to believe that you will wake up every day with the people who were with you the day prior. You watch them age, but do you see them growing old or ever picture them not being here?

Something changed in him the day of the party. When I came back home a few weeks later for Thanksgiving, he seemed to be happy and much more appreciative of life. We drank together, legally, for the first time. And when it was time for me to return to Virginia, he hugged me. It was so awkward that I didn't know how to respond. I eventually hugged him back and went on my way.

The hug meant a lot for me because my father wasn't a PDA type of person, and so I, too, had grown up to be like that. Even now, I'm very on edge with hugs I get from people I may just be getting to know. It's definitely a barrier, a pathology I learned from him. His ability to change meant that I could do so, too. With that hug, I felt loved.

I watch Black men criticize Black queer boys every day. And that's not to say my community is more homophobic than others or that I don't see where Black straight men affirm me, but by and large, it's not enough.

My father taught me that as much as I feel that straight Black men are often my oppressors, there are moments that I also know they can be my protectors. That the social conditioning that told us to hate our own because of sex and gender can be broken. Much like my father, my community has a second chance, one that gives their Black queer children a chance to survive an anti-Black world already against them. I get bigotry everywhere else. My father made sure I at least didn't get it at home, by using the tools he had, the best he knew how.

CHAPTER 9

LOSING HOPE

I'm going to write this in the only language I knew at the time—in my adolescent years before I had a full understanding of transphobia and the actions that feed into it. Knowing what I know now, there would've never been the misgendering, or the switching between your birth name, Jermaine, and your chosen name, Hope. There would never have been this loving you while still being fearful of being in public with you. Thankfully, even though we made those mistakes with you, our family only knew one way to raise a child—and that was with love. So, despite us not having the education or resources to fully understand what was going on with you, we always loved you, and you still found a way to love us back even more.

Oddly enough, my first memory of you is in black and white. Every time I think back to that day we first met—from the parking lot, to the benches, to everyone else there—it's all black and white. I'm not sure why my mind has done this with the memory, but maybe it's because our existence as queer people has never been black and white.

It was a hot summer day, and I could've only been about five or six at the time. We were all coming to one of those big family reunion cookouts that Nanny was famous for putting together with her brothers and sisters. We were a big family, and most of us grew up within thirty to forty-five minutes of one another. My uncle—the one I nicknamed "Uncle" that we'll learn more about a little later—always says, "Your cousins are your first set of friends," and for sure he was right.

I was holding my mother's hand as we got out of the car and began walking up toward the family—and there you were. You and about six other people were sitting on a picnic table, listening to a boom box, in your own world. I remember I couldn't stop staring at you all. I was a little boy at the time and dealing with my feelings of being different. I walked up on this table and saw a reflection of myself. Even at that very young age, I knew that your group was "different," too.

"Hey, Jermaine!" my mother said as we got close.

"Hey, Aunt Kaye." You looked at me and smiled. You were a teenage boy with a high-pitched voice that didn't match your outward appearance. I was just standing there, trying to process it all.

You all had Jheri curl type of hair at the time, and were wearing tight, ripped denim jeans and even tighter shirts. I listened as you all gossiped like the women I used to see in my mother's salon. Except, you all were boys like me. You were darker-skinned and had started wearing makeup by that time. Your best friend, Corey, was lighter-skinned, pretty built, and also had that same type of high-pitched voice.

Although y'all were sitting off to the side, away from everyone else, it wasn't because you weren't accepted or welcomed in the space. You were all a part of Nanny's sister's—my great-aunt Margaret's—crew. Nanny used to call y'all "the Jersey City Crew," which consisted of Great-aunt Margaret; her daughter, Aunt Toni; her sons, Rob, Paul, and Leonard; and my cousins Angel, Shawn, and you.

You adored my mother, and I could tell that y'all were very close. I watched you and your friends that day, too young to have a conversation but old enough to just listen. I couldn't stop staring at all of you. I mean, it was shocking, because I was a kid and I didn't know what I was looking at. However, I did know that whatever it was you all were, I felt it and knew that something about me would one day be like you, too.

Although I had G.G. around, he never spoke about his sexuality, and he even brought girls home to throw off any suspicion of him being gay. He was very much closeted when I was growing up. That's why that moment in the park stands out in my memory, and always has. There is truly something to be said about the fact that you sometimes can't see yourself if you can't see other people like you existing, thriving, working. I can only imagine the courage it took for you to be yourself.

Even though you had a safe home to go to, the world was not a safe place for people like you.

It's been years since your passing, and the world still isn't a safe and accepting place for trans people. Some days I fear it may never be. But the difference between then and now is that I do my best to fight for folks like you every day.

Throughout the years, I would continue to see you at family gatherings with "the Jersey City Crew," where you sometimes brought Corey along. Each time I would see you, though, something would change. It started with the clothes. You began coming to family gatherings wearing dresses. No one would ever say anything derogatory, though.

The dresses were followed by the fingernails and then the wigs. Each time I would see you, your voice would become a little bit more feminine, as did your features. From the slender young man I first met that day in the park, you developed into the fun-loving, smart young woman that you always knew you were. The woman I felt you were from the first time I laid eyes on you.

Secretly, I wanted to be like you. When one is a child that grows up with the feelings of both femininity and masculinity and no space to process them, one tends to go with the best possible reflection of oneself. For me, that was you. I was unsure if I was a boy or a girl or a science project, but I knew you existed, which meant that I, too, existed out there somewhere in whatever form that may be.

Story time again. Then I'll get back to talking to you, my cuz.

"Jermaine now wants to go by Hope," Nanny stated while we were on the porch one day. I had to be about fourteen when we all were having this discussion prior to another one of Nanny's famous family cookouts.

"Hope?" my mother asked.

"Yes. Jermaine has changed his name to Hope Loretta Cureton."

The family exclaimed in unison, "Loretta!!!" It scared all the birds out of the trees.

I remember someone saying, "Lord, if Loretta was here, she would whoop Jermaine's ass for that one." But then they all started laughing.

I asked who Loretta was. It got a little silent for a second. Then my mom explained, "Loretta was Aunt Margaret's daughter who died at a young age from an asthma attack. That's Jermaine's mother."

"Go in the house and get the picture album," Nanny told me. "I think I have a picture of Loretta." I ran into her living room and grabbed a few of the albums before returning to the porch. I handed her the books, and she began to go through them, smiling at all the old memories as she turned the pages.

"This is Loretta," she said finally. It was a picture of my aunt sitting on a car hood with my mother sitting next to her. They looked similar and were both grinning.

"That damn Loretta was my best friend. We used to be together all the time back then," my mom said. I found out that day that my mother was also Jermaine's godmother—meaning in the event of Loretta's death, my mother had been prepared to take responsibility for raising him.

God-parenting is taken very seriously in the Black community, and in my family, many of us attach legal paperwork to the title. Although she didn't raise him, my mother talked to Jermaine regularly. She would get him gifts on his birthday and Christmas. They really loved each other. My mother took the responsibility seriously.

I remember her saying, "Well, if Jermaine wants to go by Hope, then we will call HER Hope."

Nanny scoffed a bit at the idea. "I ain't calling him no damn Hope. That's Jermaine."

But my mother and her sisters just looked at Nanny with that "cut it the hell out" face. My grandmother was old school and although she loved hard, she was resistant to some of the changes. Partly because she didn't fully understand what was going on. Partly because she understood the danger society posed to people who didn't fit a norm, and she wanted us all to be safe no matter who we were. But mainly she was stubborn and only wanted things on her terms.

The Jersey City Crew arrived later that afternoon like they usually did: with a case of beer, money to play cards, and a readiness to shit-talk. Hope got out the car and I said, "Hey, Jermai— Hope."

She smiled and said, "Hey, Matt! Give me a hug, baby," and I did.

When Nanny first saw Hope, she made a face. "What's this about you not being Jermaine anymore?"

Hope replied in jest, "Aunt Louise, I'm a woman, and I wanted a name that fit me. So I chose Hope."

"You need some damn Hope," Nanny said back. We all laughed hard at that, Hope especially. "Well, I'm a call you Hope then, but I may call you Jermaine still. I been knowing you since you was in diapers as Jermaine, so it's gonna take me a little time now. I'm old."

Hope smiled and said, "I answer to both Aunt Lou."

"Okay, baby, now let me hug ya," Nanny said.

Nanny always had bite. She was definitely not a person who was more bark than her bite. She just sometimes also needed to bark to get it out of her system. It was her way of processing and still getting her voice heard. It was a great day for all of us. My aunts were all hyping Hope up with "Okay, Ms. Hope" and "I see you, Hope." As confused and unsure as we were, we were also proud.

Okay, cuz, I'm back to giving you your flowers now, so listen up. I was proud of how strong you were to make that decision to transition, knowing that society is no safe space to live in that existence. I wish that I could have been that proud to live as I was back then, but I wasn't. I was fearful of what people would think of seeing me with someone like you. I was already dealing with enough antagonism about my own sexuality. At fourteen, I wasn't fully prepared to be in public with you.

But because of you, I knew that I existed. I also knew by this point in my early teens that I wasn't going to be transgender. But that also meant that somewhere out there, there were people like me. Being queer is a journey. One that is ever changing as identities that were once in the dark come to light. As relationships that once needed to be hidden come to a place of greater visibility.

So, my journey looks something like this: As a young boy I was effeminate and figured that I was supposed to be a girl—because I liked girl things and had girl mannerisms. That was all I could process from the age of five until I was about twelve, because I didn't have a full vocabulary for gender and sexuality. My daydreams didn't feature me as a boy, but as a girl named Dominique—after Dominique Dawes, the gymnast I wished I were.

My belief that I was supposed to be a girl also correlated heavily with my attraction to other boys. Girls liked boys. I didn't know that boys could like boys. At that time, the only representation I had of what happened when a boy liked a boy was watching my cousin transitioning.

Which then led me to think that I might possibly be transgender. I thought that meant "a boy who wanted to be a girl" and you were the physical representation of what that looked like. For many of my younger years, I did have the mind-set that one day I would likely transition to a girl.

That all changed for me by the time I was in high school. I had begun to sneak-watch *Real Sex* and *Queer as Folk*. Although these shows mainly depicted white gays, they still gave me context for a culture that I wasn't as aware of, and representation to know I wasn't alone in my effeminate nature.

My journey led to me knowing that I am gay. I was a boy who liked other boys and eventually became a man who liked other men . . . and then I grew to like even more identities. The older I got, the less concerned I became about specific labels and the more in tune with what I actually liked. My attraction to trans people and others represented in the letters across the LGBTQIAP+ acronym have led me to my identity as queer. A label that is most encompassing of all that I am and hope to be. The boy who knew he was "different" now stands proudly knowing he is queer.

Back then though, Hope, you knew I was different, and although we never spoke much about it, you would do little things to indicate that you knew. "Always remember, Matt, CoverGirl doesn't CoverBoy," you said that day at the cookout. I laughed so damn hard as I watched you apply your makeup before going back outside to be in the summer heat. Your best friend, Corey, was also there, but now she was going by "Cookie." You two were the funniest things at every cookout, and we would all sit around to hear you tell stories.

The stories were always about your escapades in dating and going to the club and whatever else you were doing. I remember my mom used to worry because some of the stories covered a little bit of sex and some of the issues you ran into with men. There was always some story about how men wanted to mess with y'all, but only in secret. How y'all would get nice things from men who publicly dated heterosexual women, and how y'all would laugh when you saw them out, because you knew these men's truth.

Growing up with transgender people in our family was a norm for us, but an experience I haven't heard from many others. Nanny and my mother often say it just runs in our family. When I think about the number of queer people in my family, I remember the arguments people have about whether you are born queer or grow into it. I think the funniest part about that argument is that it doesn't matter if queerness is by birth or by choice. It is who you are, and no one should have the right to change that. I'm glad our family never tried to do that either.

By the time I went away to college, I wasn't coming home as often anymore, so I didn't really see you unless I was there for the family cookout. It was always love, though. I had even gotten to a place where I was comfortable being in public with you. "Run me to the store, Matt!" was your line over those years.

I didn't know then why you always wanted me to

take you to the store, but I can see now. You knew who I was even if I didn't know who I was, and that was *our* time. Two souls that understood fully what it meant to be different and the need to have a space where we could just be with each other. Laughing and joking as we went to the neighborhood Walgreens to get your cigarettes—them damn Virginia Slims.

As the years went on, though, the laughs became fewer and fewer. As were your appearances at the family cookouts. You had gotten "sick," as the family would say. Some claimed it was the breast implants that leaked into your blood. Some say it was the back-alley doctors who gave you bad hormone shots for all those years. Deep down, I think we all knew what it was. An epidemic that still harms our people every day.

The last time I saw you was at Nanny's house. You had gotten up enough strength to travel to the cook-out, but you couldn't be outside. You sat on Nanny's couch, but you'd experienced significant weight loss and so your face was a little sunken in. I remember I wanted to cry. I remember being scared, wondering if your plight would also be mine one day. Even though we all knew the end was near, you kept talking shit and telling those damn jokes. And we all sat with you and just laughed and laughed. We knew that would be our last laugh with Hope, despite holding out hope that you would survive.

I was living in Richmond, Virginia, when I got that call. In my mind, though, I already knew you were gone. I had a dream about you, which I'd never had before. We often talk in Black culture about how when a person is about to transition into the afterlife, they start to visit you in your dreams to have that talk with you that they are unable to have in person. The night you "visited" me, our talk was simple and beautiful. You told me that I was your brother, and that you were going to be okay.

The final story surrounding your death is one that I replay in my mind over and over. The family was called to Aunt Margaret's house in Jersey City. You lie in the bed, breathing very shallowly but still in very good spirits. Family members and friends surrounded the bed and sat beside you. The room started to get loud with talking and Nanny had had enough.

"That's it, everybody get out the room," she exclaimed. Even though Aunt Margaret had been your main provider since your mother's death, Nanny looked at her and said, "You need to get out, too!" And Aunt Margaret did.

Nanny moved her chair up to the side of the bed and looked you directly in the face and said, "All right, Hope. This is your mean aunt Louise. I kicked everyone out of the room because they were too loud. It's time for you to rest."

And rest is what you finally got to do. A woman whose life had always been full of ups and downs and downs and downs finally got to lay her burdens down.

You taught me a lot about myself and that an LGBTQIAP+ community *did* exist. You died in your early thirties. That's not okay.

Death has a way of bringing about new life. I fight very hard for myself and my community because I have seen firsthand what the destruction of it looks like. A Blackness that can't tolerate and protect queerness. A white society wanting to destroy us all. You gave hope to me, living as the person you wanted to be, dying as the person you wanted to be.

I miss you a lot. Especially when I see your community continue to face violence for simply existing.

However, there is beauty in knowing that whichever way I go, I was here, and I left here being myself. A lesson I learned from you and your journey. Your story will now live on forever through my words, so that whoever may read them can know they exist because you existed.

DEAR MOMMY,

It's so hard to put into words what you mean to me. You are literally the strongest person I know. You are a protector and also a provider. You are the one phone call I always knew I could make, no matter the situation. You pray for me, give me advice when I need it, and go above and beyond the duties of a mother whenever necessary.

As a kid, people used to say I was your twin. "Little K" was the nickname some would call me. I'm sure my being your first child was a lot for you. You can have all the experience in the world of helping raise your brothers and sisters, nieces and nephews, but it is something different when you become the primary caregiver of someone else.

The world gives you no breaks as a Black woman. I know it was likely even harder raising a Black queer kid in a society that already makes it difficult to raise a Black child without the additional marginalization. I know you knew from a very young age that I was going to be queer. From early on, you were putting the pieces in place to ensure that I had the community I would need when I got older. Making my godmother Aunt

Audrey, who *just so happened* to be a lesbian, caused interesting conversations in the family, I'm sure, lol. But you always seem to know what's best. And once again, you made the right decision.

I remember the first time I thought I was going to lose you. There were a bunch of visitors in and out the house, more than usual. I was about ten, old enough to know something was going on. I remember coming out of my bedroom to find you in the living room talking to Aunt Darlene. You could see by my face that I was panicking, and you asked me what was up. I ran into your lap crying and said, "I just want to know what's wrong with you."

About a week later, when picking us up from Nanny's house, you put me and Garrett in the car and before you pulled off to take us home, you said, "I don't want y'all to worry, but I have to go to the hospital to have brain surgery. But everything is going to be okay. Okay?" We both said okay. Knowing what I was feeling, I can only imagine what you were going through. Telling us everything was going to be okay, although the doctors had told you the risks were much higher.

On the day of your surgery, I sat in school thinking about you and wondering if you'd made it through. Not only did you survive, but you went right back to business as usual as soon as you possibly could. You didn't want to be waited on hand and foot. You didn't stop life. You picked up the pieces and learned to walk and talk again. Watching you and knowing that I come from you is what has given me the strength to face every obstacle thrown my way.

There were times I'm sure you worried about what was going on with me, and didn't know how to ask me about it. Times you probably wanted me to be comfortable enough to just say it. I regret not telling you a lot earlier that I was having feelings toward boys, because you definitely made the space available for it. There was no time when I didn't feel safe in your presence or that I couldn't talk to you. It was all me. Know that you did everything you could to provide the best environment a kid like me could need.

I can only remember one point of real contention I've ever had with you. You were adamant that I wouldn't go into the haircare business. Even though I was really good at it. As an adult, I can totally understand that many of the choices you made for me were out of safety, not the denial of my personality. The world was an unsafe place for a kid like me. And honestly, had I really wanted to go into hair as an adult, I don't think you would've even blinked. Especially knowing that your brother, "Uncle," worked side by side with you as a barber and a hairstylist.

I remember the times you let your bills go late because I was behind on mine. So, you would scrape together what you had to ensure that I didn't go without, especially while in college. And when I came out to you that day on the phone in tears at the age of twenty-five, you didn't miss a beat. You told me that being gay would never be seen as a disappointment to the family. That your only concern was that I stayed safe and made good decisions. I wish I would've listened to that last part more, but I wouldn't change my path for the world.

My scariest memory is getting that call back in 2015 from Aunt Sarah, telling me that you had a brain aneurysm and that I needed to get to Jersey immediately. I cried all three hours of the drive from Maryland. I remember getting there and finding you still in good spirits. You were about to have another major brain surgery, but your concern was that Garrett and I weren't worrying.

Once again, you came out of surgery and by the next day, you were fighting to get back to yourself. That day would also be the first day that I ever had to feed you. In that moment, it was bittersweet. But now looking back, it was just beautiful. To be able to take care of the woman who had done so much for me throughout my life. The woman who nursed me as a child and nurtured me as an adult. The woman who I continue to work so very hard for so that you'll always be proud of me (and hopefully, not have to work anymore).

Thank you for always being there for me, then and now. Thank you for never making me feel like anything was wrong with me, and always reassuring me that I was perfectly made for this journey. I love you.

CHAPTER 10

A LESSON BEFORE DYING

This is likely the hardest chapter I'll ever write. And frankly, I'm not even sure if it fits with the themes of Blackness or queerness or critical race theory in this book—nor do I really care. This chapter is the most important one because there is no solution. There is no happy ending. It's the hardest lesson we all have to learn about love and loss. No one's days are infinite, and I can't keep anyone here forever.

*   *   *

Nanny was never too shy to say what was on her mind. She got to a place in her life where she was simply unfiltered—and knowing her life story, she had rightfully earned that spot. As I've said, Nanny grew up as the youngest of thirteen children. When she was a baby, she lost two brothers and a sister to a house fire. Throughout the years, she would lose more brothers and sisters. And although she was the baby, she was always the leader of the group. She didn't know how *not* to lead and did a damn good job holding that position down.

By the start of this particular story, we were all teenagers. Well, at least Little Rall, Rasul, and my cousin Thomas were. Thomas was my uncle Bobby's son that lived in Jersey City who used to visit us from time to time when we were growing up. Thomas was always a joy to be around, and always had some crazy story about what was going on in the projects of Jersey City. He had now moved to Plainfield and stayed with Nanny. I was either twelve or thirteen and Garrett was nearly ten years old at the time.

By now we had left the "Big House" and Nanny had moved to the other side of town, living with my aunt Sarah and aunt Munch again in a split-level house on Lewis Avenue—still in Plainfield, though. The house wasn't as big as the Big House but it worked just as well. It had a big backyard and side yard and was in a very quiet neighborhood.

We all used to congregate there after school, just like we used to do at the Big House. The teen years were interesting for us because it meant we had no real adult supervision most days. Little Rall and Thomas were put in charge of the house, which meant that no one was really in charge of the house. We would sneak and drink liquor from the liquor cart and refill the bottles with water. My aunts didn't often drink the old stuff sitting in the cabinet, so they never noticed. We would watch the inappropriate channels on the cable box, curse, and do everything we had no business doing. It was a house of puberty. There were high fives and praise from one another when we started growing pubic hair, the first sign that we were "becoming men."

Of course, it wasn't like this all the time, since my aunts and Nanny did live there. We just knew their schedules well enough to find gaps where the shenanigans could take place. This became our home away from home, and I thought it was great that we all got the chance to grow up as brothers rather than just cousins.

My favorite moment at the new house was also one of the most important life lessons I ever learned and continue to practice until this day: how to take care of my elders. It's something that I wished more of us learned as children—especially Black children, who will inevitably take on the responsibility as their parents and grandparents begin to age.

We were downstairs in the den area toward the back of the house. There was a hallway from that room that led to Nanny's room. All the cousins were there watching TV, and Nanny yelled, "Thomas, come in here really quick." Thomas got up and started walking down the hallway to Nanny's room. He opened Nanny's door and let out the biggest scream—not one of fear but more along the lines of "OMG!"

Of course, we all being nosy ran down the hallway and saw Nanny standing there in her girdle with her stockings on, needing help to get undressed. I started to laugh at Thomas's over-the-top reaction while Rall also turned away laughing. But I was used to Nanny like this.

You see, Little Rall and Thomas had just recently

started staying with Nanny again, so they weren't familiar with helping her out like I was. I had assisted my grandmother in getting dressed and undressed for years already, so it was nothing to me. For them, though, it was a shock.

Helping Nanny get ready required a few things. She couldn't always snap her girdle in the back, so you would sometimes have to help her do it. She was also a survivor of breast cancer—twice—and had to have a double mastectomy, which meant the removal of both breasts. She was a warrior, though, and her battle scars just made her a more confident person. She had these cones that she would use to fill out her bra. I would help her put them on, too, sometimes.

So, we all stood there, and Thomas goes, "Nanny, put some clothes on. I don't want to see you in your draws!" She responded, "You better get used to it. You might have to wipe my ass one day."

We all lost it at this point. She was laughing, and we were screaming with laughter. That's how it always was with us. This was family, and although she was our matriarch, at times she was just one of the boys. "Having fun with her grands," as she would say. Eventually, the laughter subsided, and I walked into the room and helped her get adjusted. I grabbed her coverall that she would wear once she got home. I believe most call them muumuus.

She thanked me and then got in the bed to watch some TV, and I went back into the other room to hang with my cousins. We all laughed about it some more as the two of them talked about how they were going to have to get used to living with her.

"You might have to wipe my ass one day."

This was a sermon. These words turned out to be greater than anything I had ever heard from her by this point in my life, and I have been carrying them with me since. There is a lot of truth in those nine words, and I'm not really sure when a family should start talking to kids and grandkids about how one day "the child becomes the parent." But for us, that was lesson number one, and I don't think any of us ever forgot it.

It made me reflect on a similar moment when I wasn't ready for that role. When I was ten, my mother had to have her first brain surgery. I remember that surgery and the months leading up to it and after it very well. She survived the surgery, but the adults didn't want us to see her like that after the procedure, so we stayed with my grandmother while she recovered. We finally got to see her a few weeks later, when she came home. I remember her having staples in the side of her head and my eyes getting big as quarters when I saw them.

She could see from our faces that we were so scared, but she assured us that she was fine. It was great to have my mother back. But what would my responsibilities be moving forward? What did a ten-year-old know about taking care of a parent? Hell, at that time, I wasn't really doing much of anything for myself besides pouring my own cereal and a few chores around the house. It wasn't time for me or my brother as children to take up that role.

My family made the decision that it wasn't the right time for the child to become the adult. My mother would be out of commission for more than six months and my grandmother and her church friends took it upon themselves to care for her. They cooked and cleaned and made sure that we got to school every day. Nanny practically moved into the guest room to take care of her. My family always seemed to make a way out of no way. Thankfully, my family ensured that us kids got to remain kids.

However, by the time I was fifteen, I would have to take up more of this caretaking role. Nanny's sister Auntie Evelyn would call on me to help her with her husband—Uncle Lester—who had a stroke and was unable to really do much for himself anymore. She would need me to run errands from time to time and would call me to come and watch him.

It was interesting at first because my aunts and uncles would all suggest that they could watch him, but she didn't want them to do it. She specifically asked me to help, and I was glad to. I remember my mom checking in with me the first time, like, "You sure you want to do this?" I told her, "Yeah, it's my uncle. I should want to help take care of him." She would drop me off over there and I would watch him for a few hours. Auntie Evelyn would pay me, and I would go back home.

It never dawned on me at the time how big a responsibility it actually was. Caring for older human beings is truly a blessing. They are our living ancestors and something they did paved a way for us to exist. It's the least that we can do to care for them.

Nanny *really* meant that we may have to wipe her ass one day.

On July 23, 2018, we all sat in the waiting room of Overlook Hospital in Summit, New Jersey. Just days before this, the doctors had said they found a mass on your brain, Nanny. It was a rare form of cancer known as glioblastoma, and they would need to do surgery to remove it. There I was, having just turned in this book with the end of this chapter written so differently. The saying you coined in jest so many years ago was now coming to fruition.

I took a week off in August to come and watch you while my mom and aunts went out of town. I was there to take you to your first round of radiation and chemotherapy treatment. I cooked your breakfast and helped you get dressed every day. Measured out your insulin and gave you your shots three times a day. I even helped you shower and I changed the potty you had by your bed. There wasn't a single time when I didn't want to do those things for you. Here was the lesson you taught twenty years ago playing out.

And in this moment, I know why this chapter defines the entire book. There would be no book without you. There would be no stories, and I wouldn't have turned out to be this person telling this story if you weren't there to guide my ship. To protect me on my journey from childhood, to adolescence, right on up to being an adult. Even in your darkest and most fearful time, you told me that your only regret was leaving us behind.

If the rest of the world could learn anything from you and this story, it is that love is an unconditional thing. That taking care of someone who took care of you is one of the most powerful and transformative things you could do on this earth. Your saving me will allow me, my words, and our story to save others, because at the end of the day, this is all about storytelling.

I remember when I signed the book deal, I kept imagining this image at the book launch event of me reading a chapter about you and you sitting there in your Sunday best, smiling like you always do. I don't know if you're going to even see the finished product.

The lesson before dying still holds true, though. Despite all I've been through on this journey as a Black queer person, I still need to find a way to leave here with no true regrets, just as you have decided to do. Although there are still more memories to make, I know our final chapter will one day come.

I sat with you right after Christmas 2018, and we planned your funeral together. There were no tears, though. It was you. In your element. Controlling the things you could still control. Your words that day were, "I've accepted that this cancer is going to take me one day. I'm not saying I'm leaving tomorrow, but I just want all my business handled."

Cancer went to one breast in the '80s and you beat it. Cancer then went to your second breast in the '90s, and you beat it again. Cancer then went to your lung in the 2000s and you beat it then. Now it's in your brain. A place where you can't fight it. But little does cancer know that you are a godly woman. So the joke is on cancer because one day you will be in a place where it can never get to you again.

I'm controlling the things in my power. I'm putting energy into the things I can change and praying about the rest. And as you said, living my life with no regrets. We still have time left here together. And we will have the memories forever. Thank you.

Janet Johnson, George, and Andrea Nelson at their high school graduation

ACT 3

TEENAGERS

CHAPTER 11

BOYS WILL BE BOYS...

I contemplated whether I would write about you now that you are dead.

Whether it was important to preserve your memory as people remembered you or if telling this story would make people look at you a different way. But a conversation I had with Aunt Sarah while preparing to write this helped me to get here. She told me that it was my duty to tell my story and the whole story. We often protect those who may have done bad things to us, despite how much it hurts us to do so.

*　*　*

I contemplated whether I would write about you now that you are dead.

But I had a conversation with Uncle about you. He was the one I was most afraid to tell what had happened between us, because I knew how protective he had always been of me. The man who taught me how to box. I thought it was too much of a burden to place on him.

But to my surprise, he said he had figured it out a while ago. And he told me not to write about it as it happened, but to think about the humanity of you. The humanity of me and what we were actually doing. Two boys lost in a society who found each other's sexuality as a home.

I contemplated whether I would write about you now that you are dead.

But I talked to all my village, including my mother and Garrett, and they told me it was okay. That this story was part of what made me who I am and how processing it helped me discover what was going on with me. That they would feel no differently about you, and that they were happy that I thought enough about their pain to tell them before I told the world. They gave me the confidence I needed to write the hardest story I would ever have to write.

I contemplated whether I would write about you now that you are dead.

Because you were Nanny's first grandchild to pass away. But I know that she loves you and that she loves me, and nothing that happened between us would ever make her feel differently about that.

So I decided to write about us now that you are dead . . .

I was about thirteen years old when it happened. It was the Christmas holiday, and everyone was home. It was a night like every other until the phone rang. There had been a fight at our grandmother's house between our cousins Ral and Rasul. They were older teenagers and unfortunately, they always seemed to find a reason to fight. Our aunts and grandmother broke up the fight, but you decided that you didn't want to stay over there for the evening. You asked if you could stay with us, which my mom said was fine.

You were a cool cousin, older by about four or five

years. You liked to laugh and play jokes and all that good stuff. You had moved in with Nanny to finish high school and grow up with the rest of your cousins. You were Uncle Bobby's only son, but y'all had a pretty estranged relationship. Back then, I didn't understand why, but now that I do, it has helped me to understand you and think about you much differently. You stood well over six feet tall and had a medium-to-slender build. You had darker skin and were attractive by most standards.

My mother left the house to go and pick you up while G and I waited excitedly for you to arrive. After you got here, we played cards, watched movies, and kept the jokes coming. We all stayed up pretty late that night, playing video games until it was time to finally go to sleep. We all went to bed in me and G's room. We had a bunk bed at the time, and G slept on the top bunk while you and I slept on the bottom.

I remember you started whispering to me. "Matt, you awake?" I said yes, and you responded, "Shhhh, you gotta be quiet."

I remember G on the top bunk saying, "What y'all talking about?"

And you going, "Shut up and go to bed!" And we all laughed.

You waited a few more minutes before asking me again, "Matt. You awake?"

This time I whispered back, "Yes."

You then spoke a little louder and said, "Garrett. Garrett!"

G didn't respond. It didn't take much for Garrett to go to sleep, and when he did fall asleep, he slept like a rock. You then asked me, "Do you feel that?"

"Yeah." But I laughed and said, "Get your hand off my butt."

You giggled. "That's not my hand."

"You're lying," I said. You then placed both hands on my hips, as we lay side by side. There was still something poking me.

You were fully erect at this point. I was nervous. "We gonna get in trouble."

"You can't tell anybody, okay?" you said. "You promise that you not gonna tell anyone?"

I promised. You then grabbed my hand and made me touch it. It was the first time I had ever touched a penis that wasn't my own. I knew what was happening wasn't supposed to happen. Cousins weren't supposed to do these things with cousins. But my body didn't react that way. My body on the inside was doing something, too.

It was that same feeling I had as a seven-year-old who knew he was different. The ten-year-old who wanted to double Dutch instead of play football. Puberty had arrived, and with it these feelings I had always feared, yet always dreamed of having. At the time, I knew that relations and relationships could only be between a boy and girl. I never even imagined a day would come when I would be able to explore what I had always felt inside. And even when I day-dreamed about it, you definitely weren't the person I thought I was going to explore with.

By now we were both touching each other. I tried my best not to enjoy it, because you were my cousin. We were crossing a line that family should never cross. But it felt so right for a boy who always felt that he was wrong. To know someone else was having those same feelings validated everything going on inside of me. I knew it wasn't fake. But the fact that we were doing it in secret also told me this wasn't something anyone would accept. Especially your girlfriend.

You then told me to get up and be very quiet—that

we were going to go downstairs for a few minutes. I was nervous, and you could tell. You kept saying, "Matt, it's fine. Trust me. You know I wouldn't do anything to hurt you." Up until this point, you *hadn't* done anything to hurt me and were, in fact, one of my closer cousins. I adored you. I knew you would fight anyone who tried to cross me. You were well known for your fighting prowess because people would often call you gay, too, despite dating girls all your life.

I finally got up from the bed and you soon followed. We both quietly headed down the steps to my basement. Now, the basement wasn't like a cellar. It was a fully finished and renovated area with a big screen TV, couches, and a full bar. It was known as the rec room, where my family would host parties and gatherings.

You put the TV on, not too loudly but enough so that we could hear it. You turned it to BET, where they would play music videos from midnight to six a.m. It was about three a.m. when we both sat down on the couch to watch. I was silent, still nervous. I had never done anything sexual with anyone up until that point, despite my friends in school all talking about losing their virginity.

We sat there for about ten minutes before you finally stood up. You then had me stand up with you. At this time, you were much taller than me, probably by about a good foot. You told me to take off my pajama pants, which I did. You then took off your shorts, followed by your boxers. There you stood in front of me fully erect and said, "Taste it." At first, I laughed and refused. But then you said, "Come on, Matt, taste it. This is what boys like us do when we like each other." I finally listened to you.

The whole time I knew it was wrong, not because I was having sexual intercourse with a guy, but that you were my family. I only did that for about forty-five seconds before you had me stop. Then you got down on your knees and told me to close my eyes. That's when you began oral sex on me as well. It was the strangest feeling in the world. Unfortunately, I didn't have a handbook to learn sexuality as a queer boy. My crash course was happening right in front of me, and despite the guilt I was feeling, there was also a euphoria. Things were happening to me that I couldn't explain. Feelings and emotions I had not known existed.

After a minute or so, you stopped. You then laid

me on the ground and got on top of me. You began humping me—back and forth, back and forth—never penetrating me, though. It was just our bodies on top of each other going back and forth for several minutes while the music on the TV played in the background.

Aretha Franklin was singing "A Rose Is Still a Rose." The irony of a song playing in the background about the deflowering of a young girl being used by a man. The irony of me lying on the basement floor.

You eventually got up off me and told me to come to the bathroom, that you wanted to show me one more thing. You turned on the light and closed the door. You began stroking yourself in front of me. I just stood there nervous because I didn't know what to expect next. You said, "Just keep watching, Matt." So I stood there and watched you for several minutes.

Then you began to moan slightly. I took a step back because I didn't know what was about to happen, and then it did. You ejaculated into the toilet in front of me. I was very unaware of what sex involved at the time—primarily because I stayed away from it. I knew I didn't like girls that way, and the first thing folks would ask you if you inquired about sex was whether "you were fucking or not." And I wasn't. We also had the bare minimum of sex education in school, so I was unaware of a lot of things.

Watching you ejaculate was shocking. I remember you telling me, "It's semen. One day when nobody is around, you should do this until you get this feeling you never felt before and bust."

I looked at you and said, "I can't do that, I'm not old enough yet."

You laughed. "Matt, you are old enough. Go ahead and try it."

By this point, fear had overcome me and so many lines had been crossed that I finally said, "I don't want to do it."

"That's cool. Come on, let's go to bed."

We went back upstairs and both went to bed. You rolled over to face the wall, and I sat there. For hours. I sat there until the sun came up, not knowing what to do or say or how I would face my parents. I finally fell asleep in the early morning. I woke up a while later, after you. You were still in bed behind me but watching TV. I rolled over and looked at you, and you said, "Remember our promise, Matt?"

"I won't tell anyone." And I didn't. That night stayed our secret.

The secrecy of the sex seemed to become my normal. Two weeks after that night, I masturbated for the first time, and you were right. I was old enough to experience that feeling of what I would later learn is called an orgasm. Despite knowing that what happened with you was wrong, I now knew that I was definitely attracted to boys. I also knew that with puberty setting in, I would have to do my best to suppress these feelings even further. I was soon a high school freshman, with sexually active teens all around me.

So, suppress is what I did. I was still me, the effeminate boy who could play sports, talk shit, and deal with mild bullying at that time. But folks could tell I wasn't into girls, no matter how hard I faked it. But I still faked it, and I was okay with being a virgin. I wasn't ready for sex, and my crash course introduction made me feel guilty rather than ready to try it with someone I didn't know.

Unfortunately, my trust would once again be broken and my will tested. This time in a high school bathroom. I remember it was about one p.m. and I had asked the teacher if I could use the restroom, just as I would any other time. I walked up the hallway to the nearest one. Because it was during class time, I was the only one in the bathroom, or so I thought.

I unzipped my pants and began to pee in the stand-up urinal in the corner. I was there for about ten seconds before I felt someone come up behind me. At first, I froze because I didn't know what was happening. He put both his hands around me and then moved down to touch my genitals. I could feel every nerve in my body start to tingle. I didn't know who was behind me, but I knew that I was being violated.

I immediately stopped peeing, turned around, and pushed him off me. It was a boy I will refer to as Evan. Although we weren't friends, I knew who he was. We were in the same grade and had taken classes together before.

I zipped up my pants and yelled, "What the fuck are you doing?"

"Yo, I'm just playing. Chill out," Evan yelled back.

"I don't play like that," I said.

"Don't tell anybody, okay?"

"I won't. Just get out of here."

Interestingly enough, this was a boy who fit in with the popular kids, even though most people used to whisper about him being gay. Other classmates even teased him one time about his sexuality, but he laughed it off and still was "one of the guys." This experience officially let me know that he was definitely not "one of the guys" and was likely someone suppressing his identity, as I was. Yet he was an assaulter. Furthermore, I realized that there were more people like me hiding in plain sight. And despite our antics to hide it, we could all see each other. Our mannerisms, our talk, just our beings were exuding something that we all knew to be different from the "norm." But we each walked around in secrecy and silence.

That experience in the bathroom completely shut me down from the idea of wanting to have sex with anyone else. It would be years before I even contemplated the idea of being vulnerable with someone. A vulnerability that I now realize was shared with you, Thomas. I originally was going to write about you from how *I* interpreted that night. From the guilty place. The place that felt like my innocence had been taken. I now know that is not completely what happened, and so the experience leaves me with more questions than answers.

I contemplated whether I would write about you now that you are dead.

But now I understand why you did what you did and how you never got to tell your story. You were looking for love just like I was looking to find someone like myself. I imagine you watched your father love and adore me for all the same reasons that he struggled to love you. I imagine that one day when you were younger, there wasn't someone there to protect you from the abuse you likely faced as a child.

If you were here today, I wouldn't hate you, because I don't hate you now. I would simply ask, "Did anyone ever hurt you? Did anyone explore things with you sexually before you were ready? Who taught you about sex in a way that you weren't ready to understand—in a way that made you think I needed to get it firsthand from you, so I would know who not to trust?"

I trusted you with my life that night because you said that you wouldn't hurt me. As much disappointment and even anger I once held for you at certain points in my life, I now feel sorrow that nobody was there to save you from whatever it was that you needed saving from. This is not to say that what you did was right. It's to say that I now understand it from a place that is not centered in my own trauma. I've created a space where I have empathy for my abuser—you—while still acknowledging I've been harmed. I don't know this for sure, but my gut tells me you, too, were a victim. And in turn you made me a victim. Violence can be a cycle like that. That night was gray, much like your life. You were a beautiful spirit and a soul taken far too young.

I'll never forget the day I got the call that you'd been killed, fighting for our cousin against some guys that were threatening her. They called you "f*****" and one by one you knocked them out until you got to the third one, whose masculinity couldn't take a loss to a "f*****," so he took your life. I remember I didn't cry. I was still hurt over that night and trying to understand what you did. I'm glad I know, though, because I'm finally able to cry for you. The little boy who wanted to be loved for his effeminate ways, just as I did.

I know how important it is to tell our story to a generation of young queer explorers who need to know your truth and mine. You were a boy who wasn't blue and for the twenty-nine years you were here, you lived in the gray. That night should've never happened that way. Your life should've never been taken so soon.

Think. The same masculinity and manhood ideology that forced you and me to hide our identities is the same masculinity and manhood ideology that got you killed. Life can be so tragic in that way. I'm now okay with ending this part of the past on this page. I can only hope this story frees someone else who may be holding guilt from an encounter with an abuser.

This story is complicated, but I don't want it to be confusing. I was an adult when I found empathy for my cousin, a choice I made in processing all that happened that night. I want to reiterate his actions were wrong, and I was a victim. It is not a requirement that you ever find empathy for an abuser. Make it a requirement to hold your abuser accountable.

CHAPTER 12

THE PROM KINGS WE NEVER WERE

"Beep . . . Beep . . . Beep . . . Beep . . . Beep . . ."

Smack.

Usually, by the fifth beep, I would figure out that I wasn't still in a dream and that it was time for me to wake up for school. I got up around 5:45 every morning, because it was also my job to get everyone else in the house up. I would get ready first, then wake my mom, then struggle to get my little brother up. My dad was always last, but he didn't have to go in to work until after everyone else.

It was September 11, 2001, the first day of my junior year of high school. By this time, I had become pretty well integrated into the fabric of my school, so I was excited to go back and start the year. As a sophomore, I had run varsity track and did varsity bowling—no, there were not a whole lot of Black kids lining up to bowl—so I was able to make acquaintances outside of the Black friend circles I had formed socially.

I was no longer a lowerclassman. There was no more of that lost look when trying to find a class. No more being nervous around upperclassmen. I was finally a junior, which meant one step closer to being a senior, which was one step closer to getting the *hell out of Plainfield!!!*

I headed out the house in my usual uniform. Short sleeve maroon polo shirt, gray dress pants, and gray Timberland boots—which are *still* at my parents' house till this day, because nothing gets thrown away. I took that quick walk up Sloane Boulevard to the main street of Park Avenue, then a walk across the road, and there I was at my stop. Right in front of St. Mark's Church, where I'd done several flea markets with Nanny on their front lawn.

The bus would come around seven thirty each day.

Then there was a fifteen-minute ride through the neighboring city of South Plainfield into Edison—passing the golf course and going through the woods until we arrived at our destination. Freshman year, this trip was pretty routine. I didn't really know anyone on the bus, so it wasn't like I had a "seatmate" or anything. It was just a normal quiet trip from home to school and back every day, looking out the window, passing time.

Now I knew the bus routine, and knew everyone who would be riding it with me. Instead of minding my business, that first day got started with gossip and small talk. The usuals were there. My friends Janae, Shombai, and a few others from the city. And then there was this boy . . .

In all my years of living in Plainfield, I had never seen him before. He was light-skinned, and his hair had waves. He was around my height, about my weight—which at the time was a whopping five foot eleven, 145 pounds soaking wet with bricks in my pocket. I was skinny, to say the least. Since he was new to the bus, I assumed he was a freshman. He kinda reminded me of me.

He sat about three rows back from me on the bus, and I remember that I just kept staring at him that first day. He would look at me and I would look at him although neither one of us spoke at first. It was a very weird feeling. It was like I was looking at someone I had always known. His mannerisms, his demeanor—I felt for the first time that I had met someone like me who was also in my age range.

All of my prior experiences had involved looking up to other people, whether it was Hope or G.G. This was something more present. This didn't feel anything like the Evan situation. It was the moment I stopped feeling like I was alone on *my* journey. That moment was very Nene to Kandi when they said, "WE SEE EACH OTHER." Plus, he was cute. Plus, he is still cute. (And he is going to read this.)

He was surveying the rows to see who was who. Minding his business while also ear hustling the conversations around him to gauge what people were talking about. I wanted to know who he was, but I for damn sure wasn't going to go out my way to ask. I was an upperclassman. And I was shy around boys until I could get a good feel for them.

When I first saw him, I had that awkward shyness. That feeling of being stuck—do I speak, do I not? I just sat. And I stared. Well, not really a full-on *stare*, but a glance and then a look-away. A stare and then an "oh shit, he sees me staring," so I would pretend I wasn't looking. Only to stare again and wonder who he was.

I felt a heat rush up my neck and into my face until my head started to sweat. I was stuck. I was already into this kid. Me, the boy who thought that all he had to do was go to class, get good grades, and do his best to blend in until he could get the hell out, was now faced with his worst fear. I was crushing.

Those fifteen minutes on the bus that day felt like fifteen hours. I couldn't stop looking back at him. I had never been so happy to get to school as I was that day. I remember jumping up and getting off the bus as fast as I could to find my friends.

I had my little girl crew that I would hang with regularly. Janet and Lee-Ann were my main friends in high school. We had several classes together and got along really well. It felt good to come back to school and have people I knew I could really count on. The girls never once questioned me about my differences. They enjoyed my one-liners—something I would become well known for in my social commentary as an adult—I was basically "reading" folks before it became a catchy phrase.

Unfortunately, this first day of school would be one that I would never forget—for another reason. It was around ten a.m. and we were in our third period classes when we heard an announcement come through the speaker: "Students, please remain in your classes until otherwise instructed." The World Trade Center had been attacked, and everything became chaotic amidst the devastation.

The next morning, the world was in a state of shock. It was like knowing that life had to go on despite the events of the day before, but not knowing exactly what that meant. My routine was the same. Up at 5:45. Shower. The long walk up to Park Avenue. The bus arrived like it did every morning, and I got on. There he was again. And there I was, looking at him and then looking down. Looking at him some more and then turning my head away. Same routine from the day before, as if nothing had changed. But it had. On September 12, I finally got the lump out of my throat to speak.

"Hi. My name is George."

"Hey, I'm Zamis."

From there we went into small talk and learned a little bit more about each other. It was the normal getting-to-know-you type of conversation. "What school did you go to before here?" and "What part of town do you live in?" Really small talk—because my palms were sweating just from gathering up the courage to speak. It was great to finally be speaking with someone who was like me—not the most masculine but not the most feminine. I guess you could say I had "butterflies." He was just a cool kid. I was just a cool kid. In that moment, we were just two cool kids, and what we "were" didn't matter.

From then on, Zamis and I became pretty good friends. We would see each other on the bus every day and talk from time to time in between classes. Because I was two grades above him, our schedules didn't quite match up so there really wasn't time to build a friendship that could be long-lasting, but what we had was good enough for me.

Despite all of this, my crush didn't go away. It was hard for me to not see him as a reflection. I knew he was likely dealing with some of the same issues around sexuality that I was. I just wish that I had been strong enough to trust in that feeling, for us to have spoken about it.

However, knowing that someone may be like you, or may share the same sexual identity as you is much different when neither of you are out. How do you just trust someone with the biggest secret in your life? What if I told him I was gay, and he said that he wasn't? What if he told all of my business to other people in school? It was holding me back.

There was one time, though, when I came close to saying it. Back then, before text messaging and GChat and social media, we all had AOL accounts and used AOL Instant Messenger. One day during my senior year, we just so happened to be on AIM together. We started discussing how our days were and what we thought about school. Typical small-talk items.

However, within the messages, there seemed to be a kind of inquisition going on. He was asking questions about dating and the prom and started getting to that question that I always dreaded having to answer. And then it came: "Are you gay?" I remember seeing the message and having that hot rushing feeling come over my body. I did what I had always done, answered how I always answered. "No, I'm not gay. Are you?"

"No."

I wish I had said yes that day. I so wanted to say

yes to him, but I knew there was no way I could ever survive a confirmation like that getting out. I had never talked to anyone about being gay. It was something I kept bottled in. Something I decided that I would deal with on my own. But sometimes I wished the right person would ask. A cousin or aunt. But that question never came. And would I even know who the right person to ask me was?

We remained friends until I graduated and moved to Virginia. He still had two more years of high school to go, and I was more concerned with getting the hell out of New Jersey and leaving any friends I had made back there. We didn't have any contact after I graduated. It seemed better that way.

It would be nearly four years until I would see him again. I was twenty years old and attending my first gay pride weekend in Washington, DC. It was the final night, a Sunday, and I was walking around looking for my friends. We were in a gay club and LeToya Luckett had just finished performing her new song, "Torn." She was a member of Destiny's Child before the group broke up—an amazing solo artist in her own right, though.

And there he was. Zae. Standing much taller now, with a little bit more size. He smiled when he saw me, and I smiled back. We walked up to each other and hugged and laughed at what we both always knew about each other, but never really said. He looked good—like, *really* good.

I remember talking for a few minutes. I believe he had relocated to Baltimore by that time. I was living in Richmond, Virginia, about two hours away from him. It was the best few minutes I had that year. We exchanged numbers, promised to keep in contact, then went on our way.

All these years later, me and Zae are still friends. We talk from time to time on Facebook and make rude jokes about each other in posts. Every time we speak, it's like high school all over again. I sometimes wonder what could have been if our paths had ever crossed at the right time. If I had been courageous enough in high school to tell him how I really felt. Or if I had been bold enough to follow up with him that one time we bumped into each other in the club.

I guess we will never know now, but that's okay. Old thoughts about what we could or couldn't have been have now been replaced with new thoughts of what we will be moving forward.

Friends? Of course, that isn't going to ever change.

Lovers? Eh, you never know.

Be bold and brave and queer. I know that's easy to say and much harder to do. I know that some people will never be able to actually exhibit their queer identity in that way for reasons of safety.

But despite the obstacles, we have the opportunity to be a blueprint. We get to make the rules and set the terms for what our love will look like for generations to come. The boxes Zae and I were forced into can no longer take away from the same rights, privileges, and access we should have. The same access we should have to express and showcase our love—better yet express and showcase ourselves.

Love who you want to love and do it unapologetically, including that face you see every day in the mirror. I deserved that kind of love. Zae deserved that kind of love. We deserved that kind of love.

We should have been prom kings.

CHAPTER 13

SETTING MYSELF FREE OR SETTING MYSELF UP?

I was lined up right beside my best friend in high school, Janet Johnson, when "Pomp and Circumstance" began to play. I had heard this song before, after years of going to see cousins and family members graduate from high school and college, but this time . . . *this time*. It was my time.

Janet and I had known each other almost our whole lives. Kinda funny how we once stood side by side as five-year-olds in a kindergarten class at Cook School and now we'd be graduating with each other, side by side. My whole class began to march into the auditorium, past all of our parents. I remember not caring about anything but getting done and heading back home to the cookout my family was having for me. Nanny was cooking, and that's all I really wanted from that day.

The graduation was just like any other. Speeches from the principal and the vice principal. A reading by the keynote speaker and of course, the speech by the valedictorian. I don't remember who our valedictorian was. But I can still hear his voice. I'll never forget how stupidly he ended his speech.

"Congrats to all the graduates, we did this one for Tupac and Biggie."

Here was a white kid referring to two murdered Black hip-hop artists at a Catholic school graduation. It was that same microaggression, the same "I wanna be down" type of stuff we often saw from white kids who wanted to participate in our culture. Today, we call them "culture vultures."

All the white students erupted in praise and excitement, while most of the Black students just sighed. It was the last moment of anti-Blackness I wanted to ever deal with at that school. My culture was a joke to them the entire time I was in high school—something that they could play with while never suffering the oppression that those who created it did.

After that foolishness, it was finally time to walk onstage and get my diploma. I remember when they called my name, I got a decent amount of applause to the shock of my family. Everyone always thought I was shy, when in reality I was far from it. The Matthew they had at home was nothing like the shady, gossipy George that many of my classmates came to love.

When the ceremony finished, we all walked outside and took pictures. Janet and I took several together as our parents spoke to one another. It was unfortunate though, because I was sure this would be the last hoorah for us. Janet was headed to Rutgers, and I was going to Virginia Union University. Important note here: She and I are still good friends. It's easy at that age to think time and distance can end friendships. It really doesn't.

A lot of people wanted me to stay in Jersey. Most of the students at the school decided to go to schools in Jersey rather than living too far from home. Ramapo, Seton Hall, Kean, Rutgers, and Fairleigh Dickinson were all on the lists for most people. I, on the other hand, had had enough of New Jersey for one lifetime. I had decided some months ago that I was going to leave home and finally be myself, or at least what I thought "myself" would look like.

I had built up this idea that my family, friends, city, and state were holding back my identity. That if I wasn't near everything I knew, and everything that knew me, I would be able to start with a fresh slate. New city, new friends, and a new understanding of who I was. Finding my happy. I was gonna be just like the people on *Queer as Folk*, living my life as an adult on my terms, but most importantly "out."

My first school of choice was the University of Tennessee. Maybe it was because their school colors included orange, or that it was over one thousand miles away from home, but I wanted to go there. I got the financial aid package and was accepted before my mother put her foot down.

"You are not going that far away. I'm okay with you leaving home, but you gotta be somewhere that I can get to you if something should happen." I remember not being too upset, because deep inside I knew she was right.

As far away as I wanted to go, I was also very scared. I had always been a person who took what I like to call "measured risks." So, going all the way to Tennessee to start my queer life was not going to happen. I admit I wouldn't have fared well in a new setting at a school that large. Furthermore, I was ready to jump headfirst into a Black community again.

The racial switch up from middle school to high school was a lot for me to deal with. It's one thing to deal with just Black kids and worry about sexual identity. It's entirely different to struggle with white kids because I was Black, *and* Black kids because I was gay. That double marginalization was a tiresome burden.

Luckily for me, my cousin had just entered college the year prior down in Virginia. Virginia Union University was a small school in Richmond, with a whole lot of history and a whole lot of Black people. It was one of the oldest Historically Black Colleges and Universities in the South.

This school was going to be my new home. Although I wanted to live on campus, Gregory Johnson had other ideas. Since my cousin was living down there and attending the school, my dad and his sister decided it would be best to get an off-campus apartment. All that running away from family, and I was going to be right back where I started. But, this felt a bit different because I hadn't had a relationship with my cousin Stephanie like I had with Rall, Rasul, and my Jersey family. So it still seemed like this would be a fresh start for me. The apartments sat right behind the school and were within walking distance of campus. The neighborhood wasn't the best, but it also wasn't the *worst*, so my dad, the cop, was okay with it.

Upon applying to the school, I received a partial presidential scholarship. This officially sealed the deal that George M. Johnson would finally be moving the fuck out of New Jersey. I wasn't leaving many friends behind, because I only had a few close ones. And by this point, we had all gotten cell phones, so we could talk once I moved. I wasn't leaving family behind either, because the city I was going to had my cousin, and Uncle and Aunt Crystal, who had relocated to Richmond some years prior.

I was going to be getting the best of both worlds. Just enough family to keep me happy. Far enough away from home for me to finally explore my newfound journey into adulthood. An adulthood that I knew was going to be lived out of the closet. But still in the closet. Let me explain.

For some reason, in my mind I had built up this idea that I was going to be free. Like I was just going to move to Virginia and be gay there, and then come home and just not be anything. I thought I was only going to have to go home a maximum of twenty days a year, so I could easily be gay the rest of my life in Virginia and just let my family find out about it eventually down the road.

These were just dreams, of course.

The brightest spot that summer was me falling in love for the first time. Beyoncé was her name. The former lead singer of Destiny's Child was finally embarking on a career of her own. Prior to this point, I had liked her but wasn't the biggest of her fans. I, too, blamed her for the breakup of Destiny's Child, a group that I loved. After hearing "Crazy in Love" throughout the summer and watching her tear up the stage every single time, I decided I would buy her album a week before I went to college.

Although I couldn't wait to escape New Jersey, her

album gave me the opportunity to escape in my mind. I would sit in my car by myself and blast her. Every song spoke to me. Her femininity was everything that I was feeling inside of me. She was just so sassy and sexy and powerful. I wanted to be her. Well, not *really* be her, but I would daydream about her. I wanted to be me, in Virginia, and dancing to her. I wanted to BE ME dancing to her.

My mother and Uncle Mack packed up the truck, and down the road we headed to Virginia. I remember thinking to myself that *This was it*. That the car would be returning back home without me. My mother sat in the front seat. She was pretty silent for most of the trip. I look back at that now and know what she was likely thinking. Worrying. Praying.

The child she had raised and protected for so many years was now going to be on his own. Just a phone call away but no longer up that short hallway. No more track meets and running to pick me up from school. Her work was somewhat done now, and she had to find out what life looked like without her oldest baby in the house.

We arrived alongside over five hundred other kids on registration day. I thought it would be much worse than it was—based on all the old episodes of *A Different World* I had studied prior to getting down there. We had one hiccup with financial aid, but it ain't an HBCU experience if your financial aid isn't fucked up at some point. We quickly got it straight, and I was officially registered.

We left the campus and headed to the apartment, which was literally less than two minutes away. I walked in and felt like I was at home. Me, a seventeen-year-old with his own apartment. It was still like we were living as adults. No supervision. No curfew. Just living life.

We unpacked the truck and set up my bed. My mom helped us get the apartment together. I remember thinking that they would likely stay the night, but they didn't. It was about six p.m. when she said they were going to get back on the road and head up to Jersey. I could tell it was hard for her to know she was leaving me there. I was scared in that moment, too. I was really doing it. I was really escaping.

She smiled and said, "I know you are not coming back home after school is done." I just laughed because she always knew me so well. She always knows me.

I was now in uncharted territory. I had Stephanie, but she turned out to be pretty much a homebody. She was also a little bit older and had plenty of different interests than mine. In those first days, I had made my schedule and was getting to learn the campus a little bit. But I felt myself struggling.

In my mind, I had built this universe far away from Jersey and everything I had known. One where I would immediately make a new group of friends who didn't know Matthew Johnson or George Johnson from New Jersey. But I got to campus and I froze. I had been in a sea of whiteness for four of the most important years of my life and my integration back into Blackness wasn't clicking for me. So, I went to class and then I went home. Every day for the whole first week.

Then I was heading out to go get something to eat one night, and my neighbor happened to be standing out front smoking a cigarette. She was crying. I think she had just gotten into an argument with her boyfriend. I asked her if she was okay.

"Yeah," she said. "I'm fine." Then she asked me if I had just moved in and I told her I was a freshman starting at Virginia Union. She laughed and said,

"Oh, I go there, too. I'm a sophomore. My name is Monique."

I introduced myself and then she said, "I know you don't know me, but can you give me a ride to the store?" Looking for any type of friendship at that point, I agreed.

I had no idea where the hell I was going, so she gave me directions. When we got in the car, I put on some oldies. I always listened to them, no matter who was with me. She laughed and busted out in a deep New York accent saying, "Oh shit, you like oldies, too!"

On our way to the store, I talked about growing up in Jersey and she talked about New York, what going to Union was like, and we quickly became friends.

When we got back, she thanked me and then went into her apartment. I went into mine. It was late, so I decided to get ready for bed.

There was a knock at the door.

I looked at my cousin and asked if she was expecting anyone. She shook her head.

Stephanie looked through the peephole and then opened the door. It was the girl from across the hall.

"Hey, I'm your neighbor, Monique. We're over here having some food and drinks if you want some." My cousin looked at me, and I nodded that we should go over.

Across the hall, we met Monique's boyfriend, Baron, and her roommate, Ivie, and their friend, Tiara. Here I was, seventeen and drinking liquor on a school night—and not having to sneak it. No refilling of liquor bottles with water. No looking over my shoulder for a parent. We sat there for hours drinking and talking. It was almost three a.m. before I went back to my apartment to get some sleep before class.

They became my crew. We would all get together every night and eat, drink, and do homework. I had a car, so I became the ride for all of us when we needed to get groceries, cigarettes, soda, or something for the munchies. We became our own little family unit. I even got a new nickname. Now I was going by MJ. Monique gave me the name with her Brooklyn bravado: "I don't like Matthew. I'm a call you MJ." Which was fine but also like, how you just gonna say you don't like my name?! I still laugh about that.

I grew closest to Tiara during that time, though.

We were like two peas in a pod. She was a brown-skinned heavyset girl from Northern Virginia. We used to ride out everywhere together. Soon it was time for homecoming, so she and I decided to go to the mall to get our outfits. We were listening to music on the way when she asked me out of the blue, "Are you gay?"

My heart immediately sank to the floor. That same fucking question and assumption I had dealt with in K-6, middle school, high school, and now in college. I looked at her and said, "No, why would you think that?"

"Oh, I mean just your mannerisms and stuff come off as gay. It's cool if you are."

I just looked forward and said, "Yeah, I'm not."

There was no magical awakening. There was no boost of courage that I thought would come with the fresh Virginia air. There *was* this boy who had always feared the consequences of coming out.

Tiara's question also made me realize something new that day. I had a longing to be perfect. To be right. To be in line with the societal norm.

As much as I wanted to lead an openly gay life, I

also didn't want to be a disappointment. Even from the little bit of knowledge I had from the treatment of gays in media, to my own experience, I knew being gay was not something that was celebrated. Coming to campus felt like it was just more of the same: questions that came off as being nosy and messy, never from a space of actually caring.

It was somewhat devastating that I had planned for so long to have my moment, and was still not ready for it. We see coming-out stories all the time. Some for the better, many for the worse. What we don't get to see is what led up to that moment. How many times a person tried to push past that barrier to get to that point.

Notice my varying confidence and discouragement throughout this chapter. Notice my confusion in how strong I was in some moments and how weak I was in others, because that is what coming out truly is. It is not a final thing. It's something that is ever occurring. You are always having to come out somewhere. Every new job. Every new city you live in. Every new person you meet, you are likely having to explain your identity.

I wanted to be gay, but on my terms. I didn't want to stick out so much. I wanted to be able to have this masculine appeal to me, yet also be a gay person. Being so visible as a gay person was the issue. It was something I couldn't control and had no grace period to accept and make my own—I couldn't defer it into eternity like a student loan. Meaning, people were going to call me gay whether I accepted it or not. Some of us are pressured into acceptance of an identity before we are fully ready to accept it ourselves.

I remember getting back to my apartment that day and walking straight into my room and closing the door. I put Beyoncé's *Dangerously in Love* in the CD player and lay on my bed. It was a nice September day, but I didn't want to be outside. I wanted to be alone. The escape plan I had built up for all this time had been destroyed in one conversation just a few weeks into my new life. Matthew was a sissy. George was a faggot. MJ was gay. All three were me.

There is an old saying that talks about how "the thing you are trying to hide is usually what you give off the most." All those years of thinking I was hiding something, and it was the most obvious thing people knew about me as soon as I entered the room and opened my mouth. That day was the day I realized I couldn't escape the person I was, because I was going to be me whether I acknowledged it or not. So, I lay there. Listened to Beyoncé on repeat. And accepted that one day, my response to the question "Are you gay?" would be "Yes."

Just not today.

Spring 2006 line of the Gamma chapter of Alpha Phi Alpha. Left to right: Wayne Hairston, Charles Mercer, Gerald Carey, David Preston, Kenneth B. Staley II, Travon Robinson, George M. Johnson, Dimetrius Simon, and Kristopher Bumbray

ACT 4

FRIENDS

CHAPTER 14

CAUGHT IN A HAZE

I was depressed at the start of second semester. I had made friends, gotten a 3.1 my first semester, and was having fun, but deep down inside, I hated myself. I got up every day and still wasn't the person I wanted to be. I wanted to have the friendships and the good grades and the parties, but as a gay person. Not as this guy who was petrified of having sex out of fear that someone would find out. I was depressed without even knowing what depression was.

So, I essentially gave up. Gave up on going to class.

Gave up on coming out as gay. I was empty and feeling nothing. During that semester, I got a part-time job at Ruby Tuesday making decent money. When I would get home, I would meet up with Baron and our friend Syd, and we would go smoke weed and play basketball. I was smoking up to three blunts a day, working, partying, drinking, and not going to class. I was what one would call "smoked out" and it showed.

By the end of the semester, I had failed two classes, passed one, and got an Incomplete in another. My GPA dropped below a 3.0, and I lost my scholarship. That summer, I called my mom and told her that I was thinking about coming home, for good. I thought I knew what she was going to say: "What time do you need me to come get you?" But she didn't. She talked to me about how I had to tough this one out and figure it out on my own.

That summer gave me time to refocus. I had always been smart. I had always gotten good grades, and I honestly had forgotten how happy good grades made me feel. I was so concerned that first year with finding myself while outside the constraints of home that I lost the parts of myself that I liked. I liked being a bit of a bookworm. I liked being considered the smart person in the room. These weren't things I should've been straying away from.

I got back to school that next semester more motivated than ever to correct the wrongs of the one prior. The first was my weed habit, which had grown out of control. Purple haze, as it's called, was my favorite vice. The weed made everything less real. All the depression, the anger I was feeling. The weed also allowed me to be in the room with others who didn't care that I was hiding my sexuality. It was my masculinity coping mechanism. All the hood boys smoked, and so did I.

I significantly cut down on the weed smoking from daily hits to only once every few weeks. Being high all the time wasn't my thing anymore. Nor was I chasing the environments that involved it. I wanted to have control over my vice, not let it control me. My days became pretty simple after that. I would go to class in the mornings, go to work at night, and come home. Do my homework and repeat. It wasn't perfect, but it worked for me. I got to still be MJ to the crew, George to the campus, and me to myself.

Then one day I was walking toward home and I could hear this loud commotion going on in "the

Square," our common area much like what folk may call a quad. It was the spring of 2005. Spring was always an important time on HBCU campuses because of the Divine Nine. The Divine Nine represents the nine Black Greek Letter organizations founded on the principles of Christianity, chivalry, friendship, sisterhood, brotherhood, and the overall fight for Blackness. Some of the greatest leaders in modern Black history were members of these various organizations. Becoming a member was essentially like becoming campus royalty.

I had been keeping my eye on a particular male organization I wanted to join, that a friend of mine happened to be in. As I walked toward the crowd, I realized there had to be at least 700 students circled around the newest initiates of Delta Sigma Theta Sorority, Inc. The Square went hysterical. People were cheering and screaming. I didn't know what I was watching at the time exactly, but I was mesmerized by it all.

The crowd got loud as the girls marched through the Square, all locked up together with arms under one another's shoulders and their chins resting on one another's backs. They marched to a certain spot in the

Square and then the Dean—the person in charge of the organization—told them to stop. The older sorors then requested that the crowd get quiet.

The Square was a redbrick patio area that sat directly in front of Henderson Center. Henderson was a two-floor building that housed our nurse's office, the cafeteria, some admin offices, and the bookstore. During campus parties in the Square, the brick walls would literally "sweat" as the liquor came out of our pores while we were dancing.

"UNLOCK," the Dean commanded.

The girls stretched out across the Square shoulder to shoulder, arms in front, elbows to the side of their hips, all facing the crowd. I stood and watched in amazement. The girls waited until they were commanded by their Dean to speak to the campus. Once the Dean made her command, you could hear the Ace (the first person in line) speak out to command the rest of the girls to speak.

"SISTERS! SPEAK!"

"Greetings to the Ladies of DELTA SIGMA THETA INNNNCCOORRPPORATED." The sorors of the organization responded with cheers.

I was standing toward the back of the crowd and

was just tall enough to see over everyone. The sorority wore red and white, and all the girls' faces were covered with masks. There were people in front of them, sending out orders. The girl at the front would hear the command and then pass it down to the girl at the end. She would make a noise to signify that she got the message passed down. It was like watching the most exciting game of telephone I had ever seen.

Each time a command was passed successfully, the girl in the front spot would command the rest of the girls on the line to speak. They would say some information in unison out loud to the campus. Each time they completed one call-and-response, they would move on to the next piece of information. It was so Black in spirit and connected to Black American culture. It was a performance, an extension of how Black folks always created their own spaces when denied access to society by white culture. We weren't allowed in white Greek fraternities and sororities, so we not only created our own but made it our own, too.

All the students were cheering their friends on, balloons in hand with numbers correlating to the spots where the girls were standing in line. This went on for over an hour. I later found out that the event was called a probate—the introduction of new members into the sorority or fraternity. They "spit" information and history, stepped, and did greetings for the older sorors by rewriting the lyrics to popular songs and replacing them with words that spoke to whom they were praising. It was one of the most electrifying things I had ever seen.

During this same semester, I befriended a guy named Lawrence who was also in the same business program that I was in. He was short, darker-skinned, and one of the smartest people I had met up to that point. We had also been placed on a campus quiz team together called the Honda Campus All-stars. It was basically like *Jeopardy!* but against sixty-four other HBCUs across the country. They would fly us out every year to compete against one another in Orlando, Florida.

Me and Lawrence got close as teammates and eventually became really great friends. I remember our friendship being interesting because he was from Detroit, deep voiced, and very masculine. Yet my being gay NEVER came up in conversation. He would be one of the only people I befriended who wasn't focused on getting an answer to that question.

As we got closer to one another, I found out that he was also part of a fraternity on campus—Alpha Phi Alpha. I would see him out and about with the brothers on campus or doing community service, and I quickly became more interested in what a fraternity could do for me. Masculinity—better yet, my lack of it—was always at the forefront of my mind. Joining a fraternity seemed like a win-win situation.

The fraternities were built on principles of masculinity. Lawrence's frat had "Aims," which were "manly deeds, scholarship, and love for all mankind." *Manly* stuck out to me. It was a stark contrast to the femininity that the sororities presented.

I decided I wanted to join Alpha Phi Alpha. I had great grades, was good-looking (at least I thought so), and would be a strong addition to the organization, should I be chosen. I also knew, based on rumors around the yard, that networking had as much to do with getting on line as being the perfect candidate. It was about who you knew and how well you showed your interest through attending fraternity programs and making yourself visible.

I saw the fraternity as an opportunity to be in a leadership position, a part of a movement bigger than myself. I was also looking for brotherhood—the ability to bond with other guys in a platonic way. For me, a fraternity meant gaining the one thing I so longed to have: a masculine ideal attached to me.

Over that spring and summer in 2005, Lawrence and I would talk about it from time to time. But it wasn't until the fall of 2005 that I finally expressed to him my interest in joining the organization. After that, I didn't hear much about it so I just kinda let it rest.

Then one night at the beginning of the next semester, I got a phone call from an unknown number at about nine thirty. "Hi, can I speak with George, please?" a guy asked nervously.

"This is George."

"Well, my name is Charles, and I think I am your line brother."

By now I knew enough about fraternity life that I wasn't sure if this was real or a prank. My heart sank. I had heard the horror stories about pledging and I wasn't no punk, but I also didn't want to be walking into a setup or an ambush. We talked on the phone for a few minutes, and then he gave me an address where I was supposed to meet him.

I told both my cousins that I had been called about being on line. They looked at me, shocked. I gave them the address and the phone number that called me. They told me to text when I got to where I was going and text when I was on my way home. This was going to be our system to make sure that I stayed safe.

I got in my car, nervous as hell. But I put on my good old trusted Anita Baker and headed to the other side of town by myself. I remember getting to the apartment building and standing outside. I called first before entering because, again, I had no idea if this was a prank or real. I still really wanted to be a part of the organization. But having heard about how people had been hurt and even killed from hazing, my guard was definitely up as I waited there. Eventually, one of the line brothers came outside to meet me.

We then walked into the apartment, where there were ten other guys, some that I knew and others I had never seen on campus before. That night we all got to know one another. Some were excited to meet me. Others were angry to have to catch the "new boy" up to speed. Apparently, they had already been meeting up secretly starting the semester before. Although they weren't officially "on line," they had been forming study groups to go over the information the brothers provided them over the holiday break. So, although I was added before the official start of the process, I was already behind on information I should've been studying.

Either way, I was excited. I was finally doing something that went against everything I had previously known. This was my quest for masculinity, and I was finally going to be able to prove just how tough I actually was. Masculinity felt necessary. I was attracted to it in other guys. Gaining masculinity almost felt like a form of self-love. I wanted to like myself. I wanted to be in love with myself.

We all bonded really hard those three months we were on line together (back then you could say that, now you have to say "membership intake process"). We were required to meet up regularly to go over information. Then present that information to the brothers on a regular basis. We don't often talk publicly about what goes on in private settings, but I can say it mirrors many of the traditions of the past.

Before 1989, pledging was what we called "above-ground." You would publicly see the boys and girls that were on line. They would meet up throughout the day on campus and follow the brothers in the fraternity and sisters in the sorority around. They would act on command for all on campus to see. It could even involve humiliation, but it was all part of the process.

Unfortunately, in 1988 a person trying to join Alpha Phi Alpha (the same frat I was interested in) was killed in a hazing incident gone wrong. A federal law against hazing was enacted to help prevent that from happening again—and most states have anti-hazing laws. But for the last fifty years or so, at least one person has died each year during a hazing in the United States, usually due to alcohol abuse. And these deaths have led to jail time, fines, and violations for all organizations and members involved. Thus my initial caution in meeting my line brothers and there being a potential pledge process involved—as everyone doesn't have that as an unwritten requirement.

A movie came out in 2017 called *Burning Sands*, which depicted what the brutality of pledging could look like for those doing the underground process at an HBCU. That process depicted is true for many, and mirrors several of the traditions of the past. Although the movie didn't give the full story, it portrayed some of the myths versus truths of the pledge process.

Throughout the intake process, we were starting to become more than just friends. We were forming a brotherhood, almost like a family. I never had a "clique" growing up. Joining the brotherhood meant I had a connection to these guys for a lifetime.

During that period "on line"—a term no longer used because of its hazing connotations—there were many highs and many lows. Much fussing and fighting and arguing, too. But we were all growing together. Some of us were hypermasculine while others weren't so much. But for some reason, it didn't matter. This was the environment that I longed for. One where my effeminate nature didn't matter, and folks could see me for the person I was. I had found that in my line brothers.

Our intake process started in January with us learning information about the fraternity and meeting with the brothers regularly to go over it. We were learning all this stuff for several reasons. First, because we needed to know the history of the organization. Second, because in order to make it through national intake, we would have to pass the national test. And finally, because we were going to have to present much of this information to the campus in a show format that included stepping, and greetings to older brothers and sororities.

We went to national intake in March. It took two weekends and was an all-day affair both times. We met with older brothers from our advising chapter over the weekends and went over the same information that we had been learning for two months in secrecy. Because of the underground process, folks on campus knew what was going on but also acted as if they didn't. After we all passed the tests, our probate was set for April 7.

During that time in between the national test and the probate, we had to speak with older brothers within our undergraduate chapter. This is a tradition that happens when you get closer to the end of your process. We were all practicing at my apartment one night when I had an older brother contact me and, of course, pull that same question I had gotten my whole life. He was on speakerphone when he shouted,

"I heard you were a gay. We don't allow that f***** shit in our chapter." My first response was, "I'm not gay, big brother, and I understand." He hung up the phone.

My line brothers stood there around me, quiet. I was mad. And when I get mad, I do what I always do. I started to cry. My line brother Gerald was the first to walk over to me. He looked at me and pulled me in for a hug. I broke down crying even more. "I'm so tired of being called that."

The rest of my line brothers finally came over and hugged me, too. "Tough it out," some of them said. "We have come too far." They were right.

To be honest, there was no point at which I was ever going to drop out or give up. When kids thought I wasn't tough enough to play football, I proved them wrong. I had been proving folks wrong my whole life. Since folks doubted me because of my sexuality, I wanted to make sure that I went even harder than a straight kid under the same circumstances. I wasn't there to be just as good. I was there to prove I was better.

Some of my brothers were hugging themselves

that night, because they were suppressing their queerness, too. Together, we became a much stronger unit. I learned that no matter what happened moving forward, these eight men would always have my back.

Finally, April 7, 2006, arrived. Our fraternity was founded in 1906, and our chapter was established by a founder of the frat in 1907—making us one of the oldest chapters in Black Greek history. I was the seven on the line. In our fraternity, seven is the jewel number, because we had seven founders.

When we arrived on campus, there had to have been a thousand people waiting for us in that Square. We locked up under one another's shoulders, chins on one another's backs, masks on, and began marching toward that Square, or at least I thought. There was one last test to pass, of course. Our older brothers placed blindfolds over our masks. We then began marching, the Ace with his arm on our Dean's shoulder, who now had to be our eyes.

I remember being extremely nervous. In addition to being nearly eighty-five degrees out that night, this was the moment we all had been waiting for. We marched until we stopped suddenly. My heart was beating really fast. I realized that we had fallen. "Deathmarching," as it's called, is not easy to do blindfolded. We got up and continued. We then walked down some stairs and around the corner where we stopped again. We were told to unlock and they took off our blindfolds.

In front of us was the light of Alpha. Like, literally the *Alpha* sign in lights. Everyone was hyping us up for the show. I felt more powerful than ever in this moment, even with the nerves and the sweating. Our Dean yelled to lock up one more time and out again we went. This time, our blindfolds were off and it was our final march to the show.

When we got to the Square, the crowd erupted. My Dean yelled for us to unlock and we did. I looked out in front of me and there was my entire village. My mother, Aunt Sarah, Aunt Munch, Uncle, cousins, Monique, Ivie, everyone. All yelling at the top of their lungs, "I SEE YOU, NUMBER SEVEN!!!"

I felt seen, not in terms of my sexuality, but in the sense that I was now at the top of a Black societal pyramid for once. I was no longer the kid worried about being picked last. I was no longer being forced into something masculine as a way to protect myself. I was defining my own masculinity. I was the center of attention for a good reason. People were rooting for me.

We went for almost two hours that night, putting on a show for the campus that included greetings, history, and stepping. Because of some bizarre thirty-minute rainstorm that came through, our probate started in the Square, then moved inside to a large room in Henderson Center and then back out to the Square. While inside, half the line unmasked and introduced themselves. Once back outside, we started at it again. Travon was standing in front of me, and I could feel my mouth go dry as fear ran through me. Despite this fear, I knew I worked too hard to mess this moment up.

When they got to me, the crowd went off. In that moment, it didn't matter if I was queer to the older brothers who questioned it throughout my process. It only mattered that whatever they felt about me, I was tough enough just like everyone else. Black Greek life in our community has symbolism. It is a sign of how tough you are. That you "crossed the burning sands" and survived to tell it. They took my mask off and I popped out to address the campus.

"WE ARE GEORGE MATTHEW JOHNSON. WE ARE FROM PLAINFIELD, NEW JERSEY. WE ARE A FINANCE MAJOR WITH A 3.3 GPA. OUR

LINE NAME IS KHALFANI, WHICH MEANS KING AND RULER. BECAUSE ALPHAS HAVE ALWAYS RUN THIS YARD AND WILL CONTINUE TO RUN THIS YARD."

That night, I proved to myself that manhood isn't a monolith. That there was a version of manhood, a version of "manly," that looked like me. It would now be on me to become a reflection of Black queer people. I wanted to become the person that future Black queer folks could look to and know that their masculinity could be defined on their own terms. I went into it all chasing masculinity. I came out realizing that there was nothing for me to chase. That the only thing left for me to do was be this person, but in my full truth. It was time for me to begin letting folk into my sexuality and my sexual space while being a member of Alpha Phi Alpha, too.

It was time for me to define me.

CHAPTER 15

LOSING MY VIRGINITY TWICE

I never daydreamed about sex with another boy. When I *did* think about sex, I was a girl having sex with a boy. I created an alter ego in my mind named Dominique that looked how I would look if I were a girl, and she would have sex with any of the boys I daydreamed about. That was the only thing that ever made sense to me, until it finally didn't. College opened my eyes to some things.

As I've said, there was not much mainstream queer representation back then, and my high school taught sexual education in a very archaic way. The whole "birds and the bees" conversation, which never really made sense to me because who the hell cared about how birds and bees were mating? Sex education was an absolute joke—and the fact that we were in Catholic school didn't help. We discussed abstinence as being the best method for contraception, of course. There were diagrams and charts and that damn banana they used to show you how to put on a condom properly.

We learned the basics about sex. What an erection was, what sperm did and how it traveled to an egg to create a baby. We learned about STIs like chlamydia, gonorrhea, and HIV. But again, surface-level information. Nothing about how these infections harm one community more than the other—especially HIV in the Black community.

We also didn't learn about sex between two men. I focused on masturbation instead of sex, primarily because I still could not imagine myself having sex with anyone else. The feelings I had were for boys, but the only encounters I'd had with boys—Thomas and Evan—weren't the same as what I had seen in love stories or pornography. Those were mostly between men and women, and they were excited and confident with each other. The porn stories were so romanticized, but the passion was there. Even the corny storylines were better than my lived experience—which consisted of no romantic love at all. So, sex with myself was going to have to suffice until I had the ability to trust myself with someone else.

That moment for me didn't come until my junior year of college. I remained a virgin until I was almost twenty-one years old, something unheard of in my family. It had been a daunting task to lie about having sex (and with a girl) to all of my heterosexual cousins. I had never seen a vagina other than in the movies, and had no desire to.

Being a member of a Greek Letter Organization has a way of shining a spotlight on you in college, opening you up to a whole population of people who may not have known you existed. One boy in particular took a liking to me and asked for my phone number. At first, I thought his interest was platonic. He was the friend of someone in my chapter, so I believed he was just being social.

As we began texting one another, it quickly escalated from a friendly conversation to an X-rated one. This was fine for me, except I wasn't quite sure who was supposed to be who in the bedroom, or if that would just play itself out. I didn't ask, because frankly, I didn't have the language at the time to know what the terms were even called. He waited until his room-mate was out of town one weekend to finally invite me over.

I arrived, and he had made us both dinner, which was cool. We talked a little before moving to the couch to watch TV. After about twenty minutes, he got closer up under my arm. This signaled to me that I was going to have to be the more "dominant" person in this encounter—based on what I knew from watching the interactions of girls with boys.

We cuddled up for a few minutes before I leaned in and we began kissing. This was actually my first time ever kissing a boy as well. I remember in that moment I was extremely nervous because I did not know what I was doing. I didn't know where it would lead. I just remember silence. I know that it felt right. It was the first time I was sharing my body with someone on *my* terms. I felt agency in that moment.

Eventually, he came up for air and said, "You're a really good kisser." I was shocked, seeing as it was my first time, but I was also too excited to care and went back in for more. As we kissed, he began unzipping my pants. It was clear to me in this moment that he wasn't new to this.

He reached his hand down and pulled out my dick. He quickly went to giving me head. I just sat back and enjoyed it as I could tell he was, too. He was also definitely experienced in what he was doing, because he went to work quite confidently. He then came up and asked me if I wanted to try on him. I said sure. I began and he said, "Watch your teeth." I didn't want to let him know I was inexperienced. So, I slowed down and took my time and luckily got into a good rhythm. He didn't know I was a virgin, and I did my best to act dominant like my favorite porn star. I was an actor, and this was my movie.

There was so much excitement running through my body. This was much more than losing my virginity. For once, I was consenting to the sexual satisfaction of my body. This moment also confirmed that sex could look how I wanted it to look. And that it could be passionate and kind, but most importantly, fun and satisfying. His body felt great in my mouth.

I came up after a while and kissed him again. We both got up and went into his bedroom, where we got completely naked. He took off his clothes and immediately lay on his stomach. I then took off my shirt, and then my boxer briefs. I got behind him. There was moonlight coming through the shades of the dark room. Two Black boys under the glow of blue moonlight. How poetic, dare I say ironic?

Now, I was scared as hell. One, because I didn't know what I was doing and clearly, he did. Two, because it was still college, and my fear of word getting out that I was inexperienced or bad in bed would have been too big of a campus rumor. Let alone that I was having sex with men *and* a friend of someone in my chapter.

For the first few minutes, we dry humped and grinded. I was behind him, with my stomach on his back as we kissed. After a few minutes of fun and games, he got up and went to his nightstand, where he pulled out a condom and some lube. He then lay down on his stomach. I knew what I had to do even if I had never done it before. I had one point of reference, though, and that was seven-plus years of watching pornography. Although the porn was heterosexual, it was enough of a reference point for me to get the job done.

I remember the condom was blue and flavored like cotton candy. I put some lube on and got him up on his knees, and I began to slide into him from behind. I tried not to force it because I imagined that it would be painful; I didn't want this moment to be painful. So I eased in, slowly, until I heard him moan.

As we moved, I could tell he was excited—I was, too, but the pride in me told me not to show it. I felt like I was in control and proud of myself for getting it right on the first try—all the while still being nervous. I wanted to stay dominant in that moment. We went at it for about fifteen minutes before I started to get that feeling. Weakness in the legs, numbness in the waist. I finally came and let out a loud moan—to the point where he asked me to quiet down for the neighbors. I pulled out of him and kissed him while he masturbated. Then, he also came.

That night was glorious. I had conquered a fear and had sex with a man on my own terms. The years of suppressing my identity and not dating or kissing had all come down to this one magical night in an apartment on the outskirts of Richmond, Virginia. I didn't want to leave, and he didn't make me. I did, however, get up to make a phone call to one of my line brothers. I left him a voicemail saying that I had finally had sex.

I then went back into his bedroom and climbed under the sheets. We both lay naked in each other's arms that night. For him, I was just a conquest of a cute frat boy on campus. For me, I was finally on my journey of sexual exploration and couldn't wait to do it again.

He and I had sex a second time two weeks later, before school let out for the summer. He went home, and I stayed in Richmond. That entire summer, however, I didn't do it again. I had several sexual encounters that involved mutual masturbation and kissing and fooling around, but I just couldn't bring myself to have penetrative sex again.

I was hesitant because I still had a lot of questions. As much as I enjoyed being on top, I wasn't sure if I always wanted to be the dominant person in the bedroom. I was still a novice at sex, and even more at gay culture and sexual positions. I wasn't sure if because I "topped" him, that meant I always had to be the top. I also wanted to try the bottom position, which I associated with being the more submissive person. (Though if you know me, that ain't ever been me.) I just needed time to reflect, and figure out if sex for me was going to be the casual hookup thing or if I was ready to now seek something more.

That next semester, I entered my senior year of college. I was promoted to be the fraternity president, becoming one of the more well-known students on campus. It was a great start to what would be a great year. By that time, I was using a dating app online called Black Gay Chat.

One night, I got a message from another boy who went to school with me. He said that he had always had a crush on me and wanted to meet up. It was the night before I headed to Jersey for my birthday, so I agreed to meet up with him as an early birthday present to myself. I got to his apartment and we both began drinking while watching TV. This lasted all of ten minutes before we started kissing and undressing each other.

He then stood up and grabbed me by the hands and led me into his bedroom. We took each other's clothes off, fast but deliberate. After, he told me to lie down on the bed. He asked me to "turn over" while he slipped a condom on himself.

My heart immediately started to race. Nervously, I asked him what he was doing, and he said, "You." I laughed at first but then told him that I had never been the bottom. He looked at me and said, "Well, that's about to change tonight."

I was extremely nervous. There is a fear, as with most things that you are doing for the first time. But this was my ass, and I was struggling to imagine someone inside me. And he was . . . large. But, I was gonna try.

I had previously topped someone who clearly enjoyed it, but he had been enjoying anal sex before I ever came along. He knew what to expect. I didn't. As an avid porn watcher, the only thing I knew about anal sex previously was that it was painful, or at least played up as such on the cameras.

Nervous and drunk, I listened and got on my stomach. He got on top and slowly inserted himself into me. It was the worst pain I think I had ever felt in my life. He then added more lube and tried again, which felt better but not by much. He began his stroking motion. Eventually, I felt a mix of pleasure with the pain.

I can't say that I didn't enjoy it, because I did. But it was painful for sure. In those few minutes though,

I can say that he was gentle. His aim wasn't to hurt me, and my aim was for him to be pleasured, too. He didn't last long inside of me, thankfully. He gave me a kiss before he pulled out. I didn't stay long, nor did I masturbate after. I was in a state of shock. I just wanted to get back home.

That next morning, me and my line brothers were planning to travel to Jersey for my birthday and I had to drive. But, I was in pain. I told them what I had done and before getting on the road, they picked up some Tylenol for me and explained, "It will take some time to get used to it." They were proud, though. I had earned another gay badge of honor like it was the Boy Scouts or something.

I was in pain for nearly three weeks following that encounter and too afraid to go to the doctor for help because I would have had to tell them I had been having anal sex. So, like most other trauma in my life, I sucked it up and dealt with the pain until my body healed. I didn't have sex for several months following that encounter.

But after a while, I got the courage to try it again, but this time I went into it much more prepared. With each time, I learned more about my body and the power to say, "No, that hurts." Sex should be pleasurable. And there are safe ways to ensure that. Like they say, *Practice makes perfect*, and I eventually got a lot of practice.

I often imagine what my first sexual experiences would have been like had I been given the ability to learn about what queer sex was when all my straight friends and classmates got to learn about what it looked like for them. My queer sexuality was one big, risky crash course, much like the other aspects of my queer existence.

There is so much danger in not providing proper education about sex to kids, especially for those who are having sex outside of the heteronormative boxes. Sure, we learned about HIV, but in a school full of white kids, it wasn't a priority. Despite the fact that Black queer people fall into the highest risk category for it, learning sex education through a white lens made me think I was just as invincible as my white classmates.

The "banana test" taught us how to properly put on a condom when none of us have a banana between our legs. Being taught sex as a way of producing children rather than as an act of pleasure stripped me and others of the ability to fully comprehend what we were getting ourselves into. I really put myself in riskier situations by not knowing what I was doing and by not having the tools, resources, or supportive community to seek that knowledge.

The risk factors for queer people engaging in sex continue to be higher than that of all other communities. We are prone to having a higher chance of contracting sexually transmitted infections. The CDC has already stated that 50 percent of Black men who have sex with men will contract HIV over their lifetime. And a quarter of Latino queer men will also contract the virus. To deny the queer community a basic sex education as teens is to perpetuate the prevalence of those statistics.

Queer folks often live a second adolescence throughout much of their adult lives because of this deprivation. I didn't explore sexuality during my teen years. I didn't have openly gay friends or mentors growing up. I didn't have the opportunity to date boys or have a boyfriend. I had to figure a lot of this shit out on my own. So the mistakes people make and the lessons they learn by exploring in their teens, I was just starting to learn as I transitioned into adulthood.

We suppress who we are during those early formative years when we *should be* learning and growing beside our straight peers, and within the safety and support of our families. The heteronormative systems in our society literally have the power to change the trajectory of our lives.

Losing my virginity twice are experiences that shaped my understanding of who I was, and how I could show up in a relationship. You don't know what you like or who you are if you allow yourself to be fit into a box that society has made for you. Learn what you like and don't like. Create the sexual environment that works best for you. Sex is a part of growth as a human regardless of gender and sexual identity. No one has the right to deny us the resources we need to properly engage with one another.

I wish I had known then what you know now. But I don't regret any of my sexual experiences. And to be honest, this was the scariest chapter for me to write. Because this chapter involves a vulnerability with the world that I'm still not sure I'm ready to share. My first experience was full of pleasure. My second was full of pain. But I went through that and have shared it so maybe you won't have to.

Will this part of my story be met with pushback? Absolutely. But I'll be damned if I don't tell it because of fear. My greatest fear is that queer teens will be left to trial and error in their sexual experience. It's worth me feeling a little embarrassed so that you all are a bit more prepared.

CHAPTER 16

DON'T KNOW WHY I DIDN'T CALL

It was Christmas break, and I was about to return to college for my final semester.

"Be safe on that road, Matt," my mother said to me as I was getting ready to leave. "Make sure you call or text me when you get home. And make sure you tell your daddy bye."

I walked down that same hallway I used to run up and down as a kid to their bedroom. "You out?" he asked.

I loved the way he said that. He always acted so

surprised that I was leaving, despite the fact that I had left home going on four years by then. I sometimes think he wished I didn't have to leave to go back to Virginia. I only got to come home a few times a year, and quiet as he keeps it, my father is very family oriented.

That holiday had been great, just as they had always been for the past twenty-one years of my life. Full of family and full of gifts. My dad was always good at making sure he got everything on the list and then some. We had Christmas dinner with all the family, Nanny leading the way with the cooking as usual. We sat around for hours watching the NBA, eating food, and drinking liquor.

But I also hated being in Jersey. The memories I have are primarily those with family, a few with friends, and many by myself. Jersey was always a reminder of how often I used to feel alone. Virginia, on the other hand, was my life now. I had built up a circle of friends that I would gather with every day. I had my fraternity brothers—specifically, my line brothers. They had become the new constant in my life. Text messages daily, phone calls nightly. We were all attached at the hip.

During the break, we were all texting and calling

one another, talking about how we got what we wanted, and what we didn't want. On Christmas Day, I called one of my favorite line brothers, Kenny. He lived in Philly. We were the only two on the line from up north. We had a really special connection. Things were just different up north. The style, the street life, the music—and we both understood it.

He got the camera he had been wanting all year. I remember talking to him on the phone, and he was just so excited about that damn camera. Usually, Kenny and I would ride home together on breaks because I had a car and Philly wasn't that far from Plainfield. That day, we were coordinating if he was going to come back with me, but he wanted to stay for the entire break. I had to go back to Virginia early because I had a job and needed to get back to work.

I talked to all of my line brothers that day. I honestly felt for the first time that I had found my happy medium. The boy who had struggled to find friends for so long finally had a whole group of people he could call his brothers. It also helped that, ironically enough, I ended up on a line with four people who were straight and four people who were gay, which you'll learn more about later.

It was such a metaphor for my life. That balance between being straight and queer. My struggle to find a place in either community. It was the space that I always needed—the one that showed me I could live and thrive in both. I didn't have to compromise my identity for the appeasement of others.

I was happy to be going back to the life I had created with these young men. It was December 28, not too cold outside but still a little winter chill. It was about ten a.m. when I finally got on the road. I remember this day so well because it was also the first time my dad ever got up out the bed to see me off.

My mother always saw me off back to school. My dad would usually yell, "You out?" And I would respond, "Yeah." And he would say, "Aite, be safe," and that was that. This time was very different. He walked up to the door. It was the first time he ever gave me a hug in my adult life. He said, "Be safe," like always and I remember it feeling so weird. But I knew that he was changing, and for the better. Maybe he sensed just how tough this day was going to get.

I got on the road and headed down the Jersey Turnpike. I used to play Black R&B music from the '60s and my go-to, *The Best of Anita Baker*. I would be in that car with my two vanilla donuts and Dunkaccino coffee, with a backup Sprite, listening to Anita. It usually took me about five hours to get down to school.

Anita's voice was blaring from my speakers. And I was singing it as loud as I could. Hitting all the notes of one of my favorite songs. That's when I got the idea to call all my line brothers. I figured that the five-hour-long trip would go much quicker if I had people to talk to.

So, I started with my Ace Wayne. We talked about thirty minutes and then I moved on to Charles. Then Gerald. Then David. Then Kenny . . .

Kenny had a street-smart mentality, was never afraid to fight if necessary, and wore a full-face beard like most folks from Philly did at that time. Although he was tough on the outside, he had a heart of gold and a sense of humor that was infectious.

Kenny also ain't never had any money and being on line was expensive. So, I covered the bill many times when it came to purchases we needed to make for the older brothers or for ourselves throughout the process. He was about a year younger than me. I was a caretaker at heart. Just as I did with my little brother, Garrett, I looked out for Kenny, too.

We liked the same music and could relate from a family perspective. He also had a license but no car, and I hated driving everywhere so he was the perfect person to hand the keys to. Come to think of it, Kenny drove my car so much he could've been on my insurance. We studied together often, and when he would have his "blow up" moments, I could always rein him back in. It was like we had grown up together.

When I was making my way back down to Virginia after school breaks, I would pick him up in Philly, switch to the passenger-side seat, hand Kenny the keys, and take my ass to sleep. Kenny loved to drive. Those road trips are what I remember best.

After I finished talking to David, something came over me in that moment and I said to myself, "Don't call Kenny right now. Wait until you get home to call him." So, I skipped over Kenny and I called Travon, who I gossiped with for two hours per usual. Then Dimetrius and finally, Kris. By this time, I was in Virginia and about forty minutes outside of Richmond. I was almost home when my phone rang.

I looked and saw that it was Gerald, which I wondered about because I had already spoken to him that day. I picked it up and all I heard was screaming. Just screaming. I said, "Calm down, what's going on?"

"Kenny is dead, Kenny is dead." Over and over.

I didn't respond with emotions immediately as much as I did with clarifying questions. "Who told you that?"

"David called me and said that he is dead."

Now, I knew that David also had a friend, or a cousin, named Kenny, so I was pretty certain that was who he was talking about. "Let me call David." I quickly dialed David and put him on speaker, as I was still driving. "Okay, what's going on?"

"Kenny died this morning. I called to talk to him about Christmas, and his cousin picked up the phone and said that he had passed away."

I remember breaking down into tears. I just kept thinking about what made me not call him that day. Maybe the universe just knew that I needed to be closer to home when I had gotten that news. I called my roommate, Travon, immediately and told him that Kenny had died, and that I would be home shortly.

Of all the traumas I had experienced in my life at

that point, death was not one of them. I had great-uncles die before, but never had I experienced the death of someone close to me, not yet. This was an emotion I didn't know how to handle. I remember getting to the apartment and two of our friends, Ari and Cine, were already there comforting Travon.

I walked over to the window and called my mother. I had to tell her that I had gotten home and also tell her about what happened to Kenny. As soon as she picked up, she could tell I wasn't okay. And I could barely get out, "Kenny died." I remember her screaming, "WHAT!" and then quickly pulling herself together and telling me how sorry she was. She knew I had never experienced something like that, and her only concern was making sure that I was okay.

My line brothers weren't just some random people to my family. My line all came home with me for my twenty-first birthday celebration. There are pictures of Kenny and my grandmother dancing together that night. My line brothers are my family. I was hurt, and my family was hurt. Not only because they knew Kenny, but also because they knew it could've very easily been any of us.

She prayed with me on the phone. That was always

our go-to whenever I was in a crisis or needed some type of healing. Prayer was always the way for me to get to that place of solace in the hardest moments in my life. I remember finally calming down and getting off the phone with her. She said she would check on me and to let her know all the details happening that week.

Within hours, my entire line was in my apartment, traveling from DC, Virginia, and Maryland so that we could all be together. We did what any group of twenty- and twenty-one-year-olds would have done and got drunk. There was a lot of love in the room, almost enough to replace the tragedy we were feeling inside.

That week changed my entire outlook on life. I was the president of our chapter at the time, so I took the lead on most of the arrangements needed for Kenny. We had a memorial service at the school. It was the first time in years that our campus experienced the death of a student. And Kenny was loved by so many. We also held a service for him in his hometown, a ritual our fraternity does when a brother passes. Many brothers there said they had never experienced the death of a person so young.

The week after Kenny's death seemed to move in slow motion as it led up to the final moment. The funeral was hard for us all. That day was about finality. But I didn't want to let go of him. I was asked to speak on behalf of the brotherhood in front of a church filled with over a thousand people. I remember the most important parts of my speech talked about how if a world can have miracles, then it must have tragedy, too.

We often talk about miracles and how they happen. How there is a way made out of no way. But we don't really talk about the opposite occurring, the damage that we are left with. The memories that we must hold on to of a person now gone. The things we wish we could have said.

That last one bothered several of my line brothers, especially those who were queer. They felt they never got a chance to talk about that with him. Little did they know, me and Kenny already had that conversation. He went to his grave knowing everything about each and every one of them.

We were on our way to the mall one day, just me and him that summer prior, and he started to inquire about us—the line brothers he thought weren't straight. "So, George, are you gay?" But this time, I didn't answer the way I usually did. Something about Kenny let me know that it was okay to tell him my truth. I took a deep breath and said, "Yeah."

By this time, I had already come out to other line brothers who also identified as gay. My coming out to them happened gradually. The first person I told was my line brother Dimetrius. He said he had a secret to tell me one night while I was staying over at his apartment. He showed me a picture and a card from his boyfriend who lived in DC. Dimetrius and I had gotten close, so he felt he could share that with me.

I looked at him and told him that I was also gay. This moment meant a lot to me. I was now officially making gay friends. Up until this point, even if I had friends that were gay, we weren't talking about it together. I was trying to keep myself safe on campus. So to now have someone who wasn't just a friend, but a line brother who I would be tied to for life, knowing that I was gay? That felt like finding home.

He then began schooling me about the community some and letting me know which of our other line brothers were also gay. I eventually would meet up with them and share my truth with them, too. So maybe it was because I had some practice with others that it made me more comfortable to tell Kenny. It was still new for me, though, because I had not talked to any of my hetero line brothers about my sexuality yet—or any hetero person at all, for that matter.

Kenny looked at me and said, "Okay."

I remember looking back like, "You sure you okay with that?"

He laughed that big laugh and said, "Nigga, I don't care about that. You my brother and I'm a always have your back." I had heard the horror stories, SEEN the horror stories, of when people come out. Whether it was as public as on *Ellen*, or from my gay line brothers telling me about the things they had dealt with.

That day, we swore each other to secrecy and discussed all the rumors about our line, who was gay and who wasn't. This happened prior to me having a full understanding of what "outing" was. Looking back on that moment, I shouldn't have done that. I shouldn't have said anything about anyone else's business, because it can have dangerous consequences. At the time, I was more concerned about our line being fully transparent with one another, but it was a poor choice on my part. Especially since it had always been a fear of mine.

It was my first experience of being myself with the very people society kept telling me would never accept me. The people in my own community I was conditioned to fear could see past my identity. Kenny was only nineteen at the time. And for a person of that age during that time, from the hood, who grew up to not have ANY issue with my sexuality? That was a miracle in my life.

That miracle had now become a tragedy. I almost got through my entire speech that day, but I was too consumed by my emotions. I stopped in the middle of a fraternity prayer and walked back to sit next to my line brothers, who were all grieving, too. We made it through the funeral and all headed to the cemetery, where it was time for us to do our final farewell. Kenny's parents decided that we should be the pallbearers—and there were exactly eight of us so it seemed the universe wanted it that way, too.

We lined up on each side of the casket in our number order. The Ace of my line called the commands out and we began to walk toward his grave. We all stood there as the reverend read the final burial prayer. "Ashes to ashes and dust to dust," he went, and I just remember being numb. I think we were all numb. We were young and experiencing loss, separately and together. Unknown to us, we began locking arms as we stood side by side. I think it was the only way for us to keep from falling apart.

I remember them lowering him into the ground. I simply stood there. People were walking away, and I just didn't want to leave. I didn't want that to be our final memory. I wanted it all to be a dream. So, I stood there looking at his casket in the ground. A friend eventually walked over and said, "It's okay, George. You can let him go."

We spent the rest of that day with his family until it was time for us to get back on the road later in the afternoon. The car ride back was silent. We were all drained, left only with the memories of our departed friend. It felt like the world was watching us grieve and all we had to lean on was one another. When we got back to Virginia, that's just what we did.

Death brings people together. His loss was unbearable, and unfortunately, like the Black community often does during trauma, there was no processing of it. There was no therapy and no healing. It was time for us to go back to school and resume life as if the tragedy had never even happened.

An older brother who saw us struggling with this one day, pulled us all aside and told us to hold on to these words forever: "You never truly get over death. It just gets easier to live with each day."

I've carried those words for more than a decade now. I've carried the idea of death for about as long, too. For me, death that day wasn't the fact that Kenny was gone. There was a death that occurred within me, too. A death that many of us suffer when we lose someone who loved us unconditionally. Death isn't just the physical body leaving this earth.

As a Black queer person, I've died hundreds of times. Will likely die hundreds more times before my physical death. That is the lesson of death, though— from death comes rebirth. A rebirth in thinking, in processing, in living.

I remember when I was known solely as Matthew Johnson and who that boy was to so many until he wasn't. His death has been slow, but ever evolving. The death of Matthew was needed for the birth of George.

More importantly, the death of all the things I was conditioned to think about my identity was needed for me to survive on my own terms. And, it wasn't about being this version of "George" or "Matthew" or "MJ" anymore. It was about realizing that whatever you called me, or however I identified, I needed to be okay with that. I saw what it looked like for people to be "slowly dying" because they never got to live in their authentic selves.

On that day I buried Kenny, I also buried the belief that I will always have time. I'm sure Kenny thought he had more time, too. Time and Death are much closer than many of us would ever like them to be.

I should've called Kenny that day. He was alive, and even if I didn't get through to him or got bad news, I should've called. I think about all the times I procrastinated "the call" throughout my life to only learn that sometimes that call will never happen. Time waits for no one, and for Black queer people, there are too many trying to steal the little bit of time we have. So, live your life.

ALL BOYS AREN'T BLUE

Five months after Kenny's death, I graduated from college. It was the greatest moment in my life at that time. My family came down to Virginia. The entire village was there to see me graduate. All the aunts and uncles and great-aunts and grandmothers, smiling from ear to ear.

Afterward, I was sitting next to my mother in the backseat of the truck my family had driven down. She grabbed me by the head and laid it on her shoulder and said, "I'm so proud of you." I didn't pull back.

I just lay there. A mother and her boy. The boy she often worried about. The boy she protected with everything she had in her. The boy who was now officially transitioning into life as an adult.

My college graduation was a celebration not just for me, but for the village. It was a celebration of all the years they got to watch me grow from the young, shy, effeminate boy into an adult. Through me, someone they helped to create, they got to celebrate the hopes and dreams that some of them didn't accomplish for themselves. The village got that college degree.

At twenty-one, I knew what it felt like to want to be in love with a boy. I knew what it felt like to experience the hardest loss in your life. I knew joy and I knew pain. I knew triumph and I knew trauma. Most importantly, I knew the road that lay ahead of me, with many more obstacles to cross and barriers to break down. And although I had lived a full life, I knew there was still a lot more life that I needed to live.

I must say that it was challenging to write a young adult memoir, especially because I didn't even know that was a thing. I should also say that writing a "memoir" and only being thirty-three years of age seemed a bit narcissistic at first. But knowing that the legacy of the book isn't about me removes nearly all of those feelings. It's for you.

There were no books for me to read in order to understand what I was going through as a kid. There were no heroes or icons to look up to and emulate. There were no road maps or guidelines for the journey. And again, because I know there wasn't and still isn't much out there, I made it my original goal to get this right.

In working on this book, I've brought to life a lot of stories involving a Black family dynamic that isn't often talked about, a family that is queer-affirming while still learning about and navigating difficult spaces. I released the deepest and darkest things about my past in the hopes that someone might see a reflection of themselves in the words and know that they are not alone, and they too can grow and thrive. And so that they may not make the many missteps I took along the road.

But the most valuable thing I hope this book will teach others, as it has taught me, is that there isn't always a solution. That sometimes some things just end the way that they end. That some processes are always going to be an ongoing thing. That the five-year-old me wasn't the fifteen-year-old me wasn't the twenty-five-year-old me and won't be the future me. That there are some things I just don't have the answer to.

But I have my story. The story that has now been told. So, if nothing else, we now have a start.

I'm always talking about how *this* queer community has the chance to be the blueprint. We get to set the stage for the next generation that will come up behind us. We don't have to be so easily accepting of the norms we were forced to follow. We get to try them out and if they don't work, create something new.

When I say I'm not "blue," I mean so much more than a color traditionally designated to represent *boy*. When I say I'm not blue, I'm referring to the blue on the police uniform my father wore. How I've watched too many in that same blue harm Black and brown people. I know for myself that although I respect my father with all my heart, it is my duty to fight against how that institution has harmed us.

When I say I'm not blue, I'm referring to the first time I saw the movie *Moonlight* and how my heart raced with the little boy Chiron, who was being chased by the others because he, too, was different.

Most importantly, when I say that I'm not blue, I mean that I have no regrets about how this all turned out. Whether this book is a bestseller or a flop, if one person is helped by my story, then it was all worth it.

The cousins. Top to bottom: Rick Forte, Little Rall Elder, Elijah Cartwright, Bernard Barnes, George, Garrett Johnson, Rasul Elder

ACKNOWLEDGMENTS

There are so many people I have to thank for the thirty-three years it took to write this book. Here goes.

To my best friends (I have several, lol) Preston, Storm, Rojan, and Ben. Thank you for always supporting my efforts. For wiping the tears away, being the shoulder to lean on, and always reminding me not to lose myself in the work and to take time to enjoy it. You all are truly more important to me than you know, and I cherish our relationships.

To my line brothers from the Spring '06 line of Gamma Chapter of Alpha Phi Alpha Fraternity, Inc., thank you for showing me brotherhood. Thank you for showing me friendship. Thank you for always picking up when I call. Y'all in the book so I don't need to say much here, lol.

A special thank-you to the brothers of Gamma Chapter as well. There are TOO many of y'all to name but know that I appreciate every relationship I have built with all of you. Y'all keep me humble and grounded.

To "The Fam": Trenise, Caressa, Myra, Patrice, Sherie, Darius, Alex. My friend group from college. It's been beautiful taking this journey with all of your support.

To "The Village": Gabe, PJ, D'Ontace, Twiggy, Reynaldo, and Kahlib. My Black queer friends in the work, who have become my family. Y'all are my brothers and I love each of you so strongly.

Thank you, Andrew, Jourdain, Corey, Maurice, and Zay for just being amazing friends and supporters in my life. Thank you, Rachel and Amanda, for also being great friends and providing support.

Thank you, Hari, for being the best writing partner and friend anyone could have. Thank you, Britni Danielle, for helping me break into this industry and showing me the ropes. Thank you, Mason, for being a great friend who has been with me daily through every step of this process. Thank you, Fred, for all you do for me and so many others. Thank you, Guy, for everything.

Thank you to my book agent, Eric Smith. You gave me the opportunity to write the story that I've always wanted. Thank you to everyone in the FSG family, especially Elizabeth Lee, Molly Ellis, Mary Van Akin, Hayley Jozwiak, and Kerry Johnson. Thank you, Joy, for taking a chance on a story that needed to be told. And to my editor, Grace! This editing process has definitely been a journey, but I have finally written the book I needed and always wanted to write, and I couldn't have done it without your help. Thanks to Charly Palmer for the gorgeous cover art, and to Cassie Gonzales for designing the book.

For my family, y'all are all up in the book so I'm a keep it short here, lol. Thank you to my siblings, Tonya, G.G., Garrett, and to my niece, Brittany. Thank you to my aunts Sarah, Munch, Crystal, Audrey, and Darlene. Thank you, Uncle and Uncle Bobby. Thank you to my cousins Rall, Rasul, Justice, Bernard, Justin, Rick, Kourtney, and Kennedy. Thank you, Mommy and Daddy. Thank you, Grandma.

And most importantly, thank you, Nanny.